Sir Francis Bryan

Henry VIII's Most
Notorious Ambassador

Sir Francis Bryan

Henry VIII's Most
Notorious Ambassador

Sarah-Beth Watkins

Winchester, UK
Washington, USA

First published by Chronos Books, 2019
Chronos Books is an imprint of John Hunt Publishing Ltd., No. 3 East St., Alresford,
Hampshire SO24 9EE, UK
office@jhpbooks.com
www.johnhuntpublishing.com
www.chronosbooks.com

For distributor details and how to order please visit the 'Ordering' section on our website.

Text copyright: Sarah-Beth Watkins 2018

ISBN: 978 1 78904 341 9
978 1 78904 342 6 (ebook)
Library of Congress Control Number: 2019931217

A CIP catalogue record for this book is available from the British Library.

Design: Stuart Davies

UK: Printed and bound by CPI Group (UK) Ltd, Croydon, CR0 4YY
US: Printed and bound by Thomson-Shore, 7300 West Joy Road, Dexter, MI 48130

We operate a distinctive and ethical publishing philosophy in
all areas of our business, from our global network of authors to
production and worldwide distribution.

Contents

Also by Sarah-Beth Watkins

Lady Katherine Knollys: The Unacknowledged Daughter
of King Henry VIII

The Tudor Brandons: Mary and Charles – Henry VIII's
Nearest & Dearest

Margaret Tudor, Queen of Scots: The Life of
King Henry VIII's Sister

Catherine of Braganza: Charles II's Restoration Queen

Anne of Cleves: Henry VIII's Unwanted Wife

The Tragic Daughters of Charles I

Ireland's Suffragettes

Books for Writers:

Telling Life's Tales

Life Coaching for Writers

The Lifestyle Writer

The Writer's Internet

Innocentia Veritas Viat Fides Circumdederunt me intimici me
(circa Regna tonat – around the throne, the thunder rolls)

Who list his wealth and ease retain,
Himself let him unknown contain.
Press not too fast in at that gate
Where the return stands by disdain,
For sure, circa Regna tonat.

The high mountains are blasted oft
When the low valley is mild and soft.
Fortune with Health stands at debate;
The fall is grievous from aloft,
And sure, circa Regna tonat.

These bloody days have broken my heart.
My lust, my youth did them depart,
And blind desire of estate.
Who hastes to climb seeks to revert.
Of truth, circa Regna tonat.

The Bell Tower showed me such sight
That in my head sticks day and night.
There did I lean out of a grate,
For all favour, glory, or might,
That yet circa Regna tonat.

By proof, I say, there did I learn:
Wit helpeth not defence too yern [eager],
Of innocency to plead or prate.
Bear low, therefore, give God the stern,
For sure, circa Regna tonat.

Sir Thomas Wyatt

Chapter One

The Makings of a Courtier

1490–1519

Sir Francis Bryan was a man of many talents; jouster, poet, rake and hell-raiser, gambler, soldier, sailor, ambassador and one of Henry VIII's closest companions. He would serve his king all of his life and unlike many of the other men who served Henry VIII he would keep his head and outlive his sovereign. Loved by some, detested by others, he navigated his way through court life and diplomatic intrigue, a man for all seasons, weathering the king's storms and steering his way to safety.

Bryan came from a family who had served the Crown for generations. His grandfather Sir Thomas Bryan was Chief Justice of the Common Pleas in the reigns of Edward IV, Richard III and Henry VII. It is not surprising then that his son, Bryan's father, Sir Thomas Bryan of Ashridge, Hertfordshire, followed his father into service and became knight of the body to Henry VII and Henry VIII who knighted him in 1497 for his part in the suppression of 2000 Cornishmen who marched on London. He would later become vice-chamberlain to Katherine of Aragon, Henry VIII's first queen.

Sir Francis' mother Lady Margaret Bryan, nee Bourchier, was descended from the Plantagenet king Edward III through her great grandmother Anne of Woodstock, Countess of Buckingham. After her mother's second marriage to Thomas Howard, 2nd Duke of Norfolk, Margaret was raised with her half siblings including Elizabeth Howard, the mother of Anne Boleyn and this connection would link her son Francis Bryan to both Anne Boleyn and Catherine Howard, two of Henry's later queens. She also committed herself to royal service as a lady-in-waiting to Katherine of Aragon and would become governess to Henry VIII's children.

Bryan's parents married around 1487. His birthdate is obscure but we can narrow it down to somewhere between 1490 and 1496 in the early years of their marriage. A first son Thomas died young but Francis as well as two daughters, Margaret and Elizabeth, would survive to adulthood. The children probably grew up at Marsworth Manor, near Cheddington, in Buckinghamshire, not far from the border with Hertfordshire, a property left to their father in their grandfather's will, who had owned the manor and the surrounding land since 1489. There had been a moated manor house at Marsworth since 1328, once granted by King Edward III to his shield-bearer, Thomas Cheney, ancestor of the Cheneys of Drayton-Beauchamp. It had been updated by the time it came to the Bryan's and as well as the manor there were outbuildings, gardens and a fish pond. It was a country retreat away from the trials of court life and an idyllic place to grow up.

As was normal children would often be raised in another household and it is possible that Bryan was sent to the household of Sir Thomas Parr of Kendal, Westmoreland, in Northamptonshire as he would later refer to him as his special patron. Sir Thomas Parr was also descended from Edward III and his family too had served their sovereigns. Parr was made a Knight of the Bath around the time of Henry VIII's coronation and was close to the new king. His home place, Kendal Castle, was in a state of disrepair and so the Parr's chose to live in Blackfriars, London, from 1512. Sir Thomas would become the father of another of Henry's queens, Katherine Parr, who was born at this time. Through all his connections Francis Bryan was well and truly linked to life at the Henrician court.

We know little of his education. Parr believed, as did Thomas More, Henry's councillor and a known humanist and philosopher, that boys and girls should be educated together and Lady Maud Parr, a well-educated lady herself, would later be responsible for running the royal school at court which taught French, Latin, philosophy, theology and the Classics. Lady Parr was fluent in French and taught all her children to read and write at a young age so we can assume that Bryan was also given a solid education during his time in their household of which he had fond memories.

Wood's *Athenae Oxonienses* indicates Bryan went to study at Oxford University but the date given in its companion volume *Alumni Oxonienses 1500–1714* sees him attending in 1522 by which time Bryan would have been at least in his mid-twenties and serving the king. Boys typically entered the college between the ages of fourteen and seventeen. We do know however that Bryan was well educated and had learnt French as his diplomatic and military career will show.

Bryan would later say that he came to Henry's court 'very young'.[1] Whether through his mother or his patron, he must have been at court frequently. Soon he was part of a close group of friends that the young king had gathered around him – his 'minions' who included Charles Brandon, Thomas Grey, Thomas Knyvett, Henry Guildford and Nicholas Carew. His sisters Margaret and Elizabeth would also attend court at an early age and both would marry the king's companions. Margaret was the first to marry being the eldest and around April 1512 she wed Henry Guildford, son of Sir Richard Guildford. It must have been a court affair as the king's sister Mary gave the couple a gift of 6s. 8d. Henry gave them manors in Byner, Lincolnshire, and Hampton-in-Arden, Warwickshire but they made their home at Benenden in Kent and later Leeds Castle.

This was the young king's heyday, full of the pleasures of what life could bring from jousting, dancing, hunting, masques and pageants. With his band of brothers around him Henry was determined to shake off the shackles of his last years with his father when it was said he was kept as close as a girl and well-guarded. But he was also determined to wage war on France

– England's ancient enemy since 1066 – in his sights from the moment he was crowned. The Venetian ambassador had described Henry as magnificent, liberal and a great enemy of the French and his minions would all take roles in the coming hostilities.

On 17 November 1511 Henry signed the Treaty of Westminster with King Ferdinand II of Aragon (Katherine of Aragon's father) which was an agreement to attack France by the end of April 1512 and war was duly declared on Henry's enemies. In August 1512, Edward Howard, the new Lord Admiral, attacked the French fleet near Bertheaume Bay. Howard headed a flotilla of twenty-five English warships in Henry's prized new ship, the *Mary Rose*, closely followed by Sir Thomas Knyvett and Sir John Carew in the *Regent* and Charles Brandon and Sir Henry Guildford in the *Sovereign*. On 10 August, the Battle of St Mathieu commenced and disaster struck.

Now the enemy had suffered no small amount of damage, and the English were not far removed from coming out on top, when in the middle of the fight, either because the despairing enemy did not wish to die unavenged, or because of some mischance, a great fire broke out on the French ship and spread to the English one. Then the fighters were surrounded by flames and quickly turned from fighting to putting out the fire. But since the ships were chained together, the fire could not be extinguished by any human power before it consumed both ships, together with their crews. This was the most piteous sight in human memory, as the fire consumed men and the water swallowed them. But most plunged into the latter to avoid the former, and a number were rescued by their mates. So the fight was equally fatal and deadly to both sides, and nobody gained the victory. More than six hundred Englishmen perished, including Thomas the ship's captain. The French losses were greater, and it is said that more than 1,000 men were lost. The reason for this great catastrophe was that because of the all-consuming flames the battle was almost ended before it began, and so neither side could come to the aid of their doomed men.[2]

Henry's close band of brothers had lost its first member, Sir Thomas Knyvett. As the king and his companions mourned, Edward Howard, Thomas's brother-in-law as well as his friend, swore to revenge his death.

In April 1513, the Lord Admiral, was in command of a twenty-four ship fleet containing 5000 sailors and 3000 soldiers sweeping the channel in preparation for continuing a new season of war with France. Bryan's first official role came as captain of the *Margaret Bonaventure*, a 120 ton supply ship capable of carrying 100 men engaged to provision the warships. There is no record of him having any naval experience before this and so to be made captain was an honour indeed but also probably one that was overseen by the ship's previous captain, Richard Berdisle.

Bryan was to meet the navy at Brest to revictual them but did not engage in the fighting that ensued days later. However the men were grateful for the supplies. Edward Echyngham reported to Wolsey:

And so we made about unto them, sailing through the Broad S[ound] 10 miles out of our course, and came into the Treade the same day, t[o the] Kyng's most royal army being in Brest water with the vytlers, in m[y] company; and then I came aboard to my lord admiral. And then I trow there was never knight more welcome to his sovereign lady [than] I was to my lord Admiral and unto all the whole army, for by [cause that] I brought the vytlers with me. For of 10 days before there was no [man] in all the army that had but one meal a day and once drink.[3]

But on 25 April 1513, disaster struck. The lord admiral launched an assault on the French flagship *Cordelière*. Boarding the vessel, his own galley came adrift, leaving Howard and his men to the mercy of the enemy's sailors. Howard threw his admiral's gold whistle overboard, a symbol of his rank, and was either forced off the ship or jumped to his death, drowning in the salty water, weighed down by his heavy armour.

Henry assuaged some of his anger by invading France. Bryan helped ferry 25,000 men to Calais in ongoing trips across the Channel. His brother-in-law, Nicholas Carew, was one of several who accompanied the king and Henry Guildford went over too commanding one hundred men of the king's ward. In June Thérouanne and Tournai were taken. The king's minions had seen their first losses and those that remained would become closer to the king.

In 1514, there were rumours that Bryan's younger sister Elizabeth, had become the king's mistress. As their mother was working in Katherine of Aragon's household it seems Bryan's younger sister was also living at court. Charles Brandon mentioned her in a letter to Henry and since he had not long married the king's sister Mary it could have all been a game of courtly love. He told Henry 'I beseech your grace to tell Mistress Blount and Mistress Carew the next time I write to them or send them tokens, they shall write to me or send me tokens again'.[4] He could have been courting Elizabeth but it is unlikely and he was probably acting as Henry's go-between seeing as Henry would definitely take Bessie Blount as his mistress.

Elizabeth would marry Nicholas Carew this year and have her first child at the tender age of thirteen. Henry attended their wedding and may have even arranged the match. He was certainly generous with his gifts to Elizabeth giving her and her new husband lands in Wallington, Mitcham, Carshalton and Woodcote worth forty marks a year to make up a part payment of fifty marks as their marriage portion, a 6s 8d wedding gift and presents of 'many beautiful diamonds and pearls and innumerable jewels'[5] which had belonged to the queen. There were also expensive presents of cloth and furs over the next two years that point to the king being enamoured of Bryan's sister although there is no definite proof she was his mistress.

There was also a story that when Francis Bryan had shown interest in one of the ladies at court who was also Henry's mistress, although unnamed, that the king 'gave over the lady ever after to him'.[6] It certainly wasn't Bessie Blount as the celebrations at New Year's Eve made clear. During a masque, the king, Charles Brandon, Nicholas Carew and Lord Fellinger partnered Bessie Blount, Bryan's sisters Margaret and Elizabeth and Lady Fellinger. There 'were four ladies in gowns, after the fashion of Savoy, of blue velvet, lined with cloth, the Velvet all to cut, and mantels like tippets knit together all of silver and on their heads bonnets of burned gold, the four torchbearers were in satin white and blue. This strange apparel pleased much every person, and in especial the Queen, and thus these four lords and four ladies came into the Queen's chamber with great light of torches, and danced a great season, and then put off their visors, and then they were well known...'[7] It was also well known that Henry had partnered Bessie throughout the performance.

Bryan and Carew were becoming firm favourites of the king's. For the May tournament of 1514 the king lent horses and armour to them both for jousting. The tilt yard at Greenwich had become Henry's permanent play area. Close to the Palace of Placentia, Henry had added extra stables, an armoury, a gallery and a five-storey tower for viewing. Such was Henry's delight in the joust the Spanish ambassador commented, 'The King of England amuses himself almost every day of the week with running the ring, and with jousts and tournaments on foot in which one single person fights with an appointed adversary... The most interested in the combats is the king himself, who never omits being present at them'.[8] The king may have excelled at the joust but Nicholas

Carew shone as the star of this tournament. He became so popular and so skilled that Henry gave him his own tilt yard at Greenwich in 1515. Carew and Bryan were both also charged with teaching the art of chivalry to 'encourage all youth to seek deeds of arms'[9] and pass on their skills to a younger generation. On 19 April 1515 there were entertainments at Richmond, jousting and a banquet, in honour of Louise of Savoy, Regent of France and the renewal of the Treaty of Paris. Signed originally in 1514, the treaty promoted peace between the two countries and included the marriage of Henry's sister Mary to the French king Louis XII who had died in January. Mary would soon be on her way home with her new husband, Charles Brandon, who for once was not at the joust. Instead Bryan and Carew rode out with the king again. Henry paid for his friends coats of blue satin embroidered with white satin including '48 yds. blue satin, at 7s. 8d. a yd., for coats, trappers and saddlery for Bryan and Carew'.[10]

For the celebration of May Day at Shooters Hill, Henry took part in a masque based on the story of Robin Hood, one of his favourite themes. Eighty-seven yards of green satin were needed for Bryan's and Carew's coats and Arnold, the queen's embroiderer, made hawthorn leaves for their headpieces. The king himself was dressed 'entirely in green velvet, cap, doublet, hose, shoes and everything'.[11] Henry had with him a band of archers and a hundred noblemen who were joined by Queen Katherine and her ladies to watch an archery contest. Afterwards Henry asked his queen whether she would 'enter the greenwood and see how the outlaws lived'[12] and when Katherine said she was content to, he led her into the woods to an area decorated with floral bowers and where tables were laid out with a feast. Bryan was also at the Christmas entertainments at Eltham when the king's chapel master William Cornysh devised a castle pageant.

For all the pleasure, there was also work to do and in 1516 Bryan became the King's cupbearer, serving him when he dined, which brought him in even closer contact to the king both officially and personally. His mother too, who had been Katherine of Aragon's lady-in-waiting, now became the newly born Princess Mary's governess, a position that earnt her £50 a year for life. Bryan's father died sometime in 1517 or 1518 and was buried at Cheddington. By the time of her next payment in 1519 his mother had remarried one David Zouche, son of John Zouche of Codnor, Derbyshire, who little is known about.

In July 1517 to mark the signing of the Treaty of Cambrai – a peace accord between France and the Holy Roman Empire – a tournament and banquet were held. Bryan jousted again on the king's side at Greenwich and was clothed at the king's cost. Sir Henry Guildford, now Master of Horse, led the king's men against Charles Brandon, the Duke of Suffolk, head of the challengers. The king and Brandon jousted that day like 'Hector and Achilles'.[13] The 'king and the duke ran fiercely together, and broke many spears, and so did all the others, that it was hard to say who did best'.[14] But Carew stole the show starring as the 'Blue Knight' and carrying a huge lance 12 feet in length, 9 inches in diameter 'to the extreme admiration and astonishment'[15] of all.

Bryan was also on the rise and in October he received a large payment of £66 13s 4d which must mean that his appointment of Master of the Toils began this year or more likely the end of 1516 to receive a year's salary rather than the often quoted 1518. As Master of the Toils he was in charge of the upkeep of Henry's hunting grounds, keeping them supplied and looking after the 'toils' – the canvas and nets used for directing and corralling deer and other game for which he was paid £33 6s 8d every half year and an extra payment every time he moved deer into the king's hunting grounds including Greenwich and Rayleigh Park.

Carew and Bryan were also stated as 'cipherers' in the records at this time which has been posited as another term for cupbearers rather than the more modern use, but as they were so close to the king they could also have been charged with working on his correspondence. Henry VII definitely used ciphers (coded letters) and Katherine of Aragon would use them to communicate with her father so it is not hard to imagine that Henry would have begun to employ people to treat his correspondence accordingly. And who best to help him write personal letters than his closest friends?

Cardinal Wolsey, a butcher's son from Suffolk who had risen to the position of Lord Chancellor, had quickly gained power at Henry's court. Educated at Magdalen College, Oxford, he was ordained around 1498 and became chaplain to the Archbishop of Canterbury and then Henry's father. In 1514 he was made Archbishop of York and was appointed both Lord Chancellor and Cardinal in 1515. He could see how close the king was to his friends and he was becoming exasperated with this band of minions and their influence over Henry. He felt they had become too close for comfort and had far too much control over their sovereign. Control that Wolsey wanted to negate. He succeeded in having Bryan's brother-in-law Nicholas Carew exiled from court but he was back by March 1518. Pace reported that 'Mr. Carew and his wife be returned to the King's grace, too soon after my opinion'.[16] Pace, as one of Wolsey's men, knew his master's thoughts on Bryan, Carew and their companions.

But Wolsey couldn't break their bond – at least not yet – and in September 1518 many of his minions were given an even closer position to the king. Bryan received £6 13s 4d as constable of Hertford castle and was made gentleman of the privy chamber – a new post – as one of Henry's closest attendants along with Nicholas Carew, William Coffin, Edward Neville, Henry Norris and Arthur Pole. But Bryan would soon be combining his role at court with more diplomatic duties.

When a French embassy arrived to sign the Treaty of London – a non-aggression pact between Europe's major powers – great celebrations ensued. Francis I had succeeded his father-in-law

Louis XII in January 1515. Bryan, as one of the king's men, was paired with one of Francis I's courtiers to attend processions and joined the French ambassadors at the joust, feasting and dancing that followed. The Venetian ambassador reported peace was proclaimed at St Paul's and afterwards:

> ... the Cardinal of York was followed by the entire company to his own dwelling, where we sat down to a most sumptuous supper, the like of which, I fancy, was never given either by Cleopatra or Caligula: the whole banqueting hall being so decorated with huge vases of gold and silver, that I fancied myself in the tower of Chosroes, where that monarch caused divine honors to be paid him. After supper, a mummery, consisting of twelve male and twelve female maskers, made their appearance in the richest and most sumptuous array, being all dressed alike. After performing certain dances, they removed their visors. The two leaders were the King and the Queen Dowager of France, and all the others were lords and ladies, who seated themselves apart from the tables, and were served with countless dishes of confections and other delicacies. Large bowls filled with ducats and dice were then placed upon the table for such as liked to gamble. Shortly after, the supper tables being removed, dancing commenced, and lasted until after midnight.[17]

A large contingent of knights and noblemen including Bryan and headed by Charles Somerset, the Earl of Worcester and the king's chamberlain, made a return visit to the court of Francis I, arriving in December. Worcester had his work cut out for him. He was commissioned to arrange the marriage of the Dauphin and Henry's daughter Princess Mary, receive the French king's oaths on the marriage of his son and the peace treaty, return Tournai on payment of 50,000 francs and discuss the problem of Scotland with him. But there was still time for pleasure and Francis I laid on many entertainments including a spectacle at the Bastille.

On 22 Dec. the banquet was held in the Bastille. The large space in its centre was squared, and floored with timber, three galleries being raised all round, one above the other; the whole being covered in with an awning of blue canvas, well waxed, which prevented the rain from penetrating. The canvas was painted to represent the heavens, and Latin and French mottoes were suspended about the hall. White and tawny cloth was hung under the galleries, and the floor was carpeted with the same. There was an immense number of torches in sconces and in chandeliers, each torch weighing three pounds, throwing a marvellous blaze of light on the starry ceiling. In the four corners of the hall were cupboards filled with gold and silver vases. The platform was overhung by a bower of evergreens. Tables were placed at the extremity of the platform, and down the sides, the guests being seated inside. Below the platform were two tables, extending the whole length of the place, at which gentlemen of the English embassy and Frenchmen were seated alternately with ladies. The company danced to trumpets and fifes till the third hour of the night. Then supper commenced, which lasted two hours, and consisted of nine courses: each course was announced by a flourish of trumpets. After supper several companies of maskers made their appearance, amongst them the King. Then came a collation of confections, served by ladies dressed in the Italian fashion, chief among whom were the daughters of Galeazzo Visconti; and by degrees the company dispersed...[18]

The spectacle was followed by a day of jousting and then Worcester and the other ambassadors got down to work but Bryan and his friends were obviously bored, taking to the streets of Paris 'throwing eggs, stones and other foolish trifles at the people'.[19] They returned home in February 1519 'all French, in eating, drinking and apparel, yea, and in French vices and brags'.[20]

Wolsey was furious to hear the reports of their bad behaviour and was still worried about Bryan and his friends influence on the king. Wolsey 'who, perceiving the aforesaid to be so intimate with the King, that in the course of time they might have ousted him from the government, anticipated them under pretence of their being youths of evil counsel'[21] and called them before the Privy Council.

> Certain young men in the king's Privy Chamber, disregarding his estate or degree, were so familiar and homely with him, and played such light touches with him that they forgot themselves: which things although the king of his gentle nature suffered and did not rebuke nor reprove of: yet the king's council thought it not suitable to be suffered for the king's honor, and therefore they altogether came to the king, beseeching him all these enormities and lightness to redress. To whom the king answered, that he had chosen his council, both for the maintenance of his honor and for the defense of all things that might blemish the same: wherefore if they saw any about him misuse themselves, he committed it to their reformation. Then the king's council called before them Nicholas Carew..... with diverse others also of the privy chamber, which had been in the French court, and banished them from the court for diverse considerations, laying nothing particularly to their charges... which discharge out of the court grieved the hearts of these young men who called the king's minions.[22]

Henry's band of friends had to leave court and were replaced by more senior men but the king missed his companions and by September they were back in favour and attending the not so subtle masque of age and youth at New Hall, near Chelmsford, Essex. Bryan was back by his king's side and it was a bright place to be.

Henry VIII

Chapter Two

To France

1520–1522

Bryan's stint at the French court had enamoured him of all things French and he was eager to accompany the king to his momentous meeting with Francis I at the Field of the Cloth of Gold between Ardres in France and Guînes in the Pale of Calais in June 1520. Wolsey wanted to follow on the Treaty of London with meetings between Henry and both Francis I and Charles V to cement the peace – the universal peace that he strived towards but that was always at risk of fracturing. Henry and Charles V, Queen Katherine's nephew, had met briefly before the English king left for Calais and they would meet again after the Field of the Cloth of Gold but for now Henry's meeting with Francis I would see nearly three weeks of jousting, feasting, drinking, pageant displays, wrestling, archery and diplomatic discussions.

Henry and Francis, both young, athletic kings, met for the first time on 7 June, galloping towards each other as if in combat before heartily embracing. Bryan was with them as they received refreshments in a small pavilion decorated with fleur-de-lys and set out the terms of their meeting. When Henry was declared king of France as part of his title he said to the French king 'I cannot be while you are here, for I would be a liar'[1] although he firmly believed France should be his.

Francis replied, 'Mon Frere, now that you are my friend, you are King of France, King of all my possessions, and of me myself; but without friendship I acknowledge no other King of France than myself, and thus, with the aid of our Lord God, do I hope to be able to defend and preserve this kingdom for myself and my successors'. To which Henry said 'Mon Frere, I swear to our

Lord God, although I have been very deeply in love, that I never had so strong a wish and desire to gratify any of my appetites, as that of seeing and embracing you, and I promise God, who has granted me this grace, never to love anybody so much as I love you; and should you ever find me fail in this love, and that I do not love you above everything, and do not perform such office as becomes a true and perfect friend, I am willing to be accounted the most base and sorry prince and gentleman in the world.'[2] Loving brothers indeed – for a few days at least. The Field of the Cloth of Gold would show an outward accord between the two kings but there would always be tensions simmering under the surface.

Henry stayed in a temporary palace whereas many of the king's entourage stayed in nearby Guînes Castle or in tents that littered the fields around. Five thousand people had accompanied the king and queen and many more had been in France since March building and organising accommodation and supplies. Henry's 'palace of illusions' covered an area of nearly 12,000 square yards with four wings surrounding a central courtyard. It was built on a brick base about eight feet high and above that the walls were made of canvas painted to look like brick and stone with glass windows. A gatehouse was added to add to the illusion and topped with symbolic lions and Cupid looking down on the proceedings. In front of the palace was a fountain dedicated to Bacchus, flowing freely with wine. Henry had had 40,000 gallons of wine shipped over for the spectacle and continuous consumption. It was said that while the men jousted the women got drunk!

The jousts were a huge part of the entertainments arranged by the Duke of Suffolk and the French Admiral, Bonnivet. Over 300 men would take part including Bryan and his friends and brothers-in-law, Nicholas Carew and Henry Guildford. Three hundred and twenty-seven staves were broken over the course of the joust[3] and both the English and French excelled in their displays of horsemanship. At one of the jousts Bryan wore a tunic 'one side of blue velvet with a man's heart burning in a ladies hand'[4] and the other side of white satin embroidered with letters of gold as he rode to the challenge. Bryan excelled being one of only nine men who achieved the highest score. He jousted on four occasions, one day running eighteen courses and breaking nine lances[5] and received grand prizes for his efforts. He also took part in a sword fighting contest where he 'fought fervently battle after battle'.[9] Each competition was a test of skill against the French – a chance to show off but with serious undertones. It showed the might of England's best fighters.

On 17 June the two kings visited each other's wives. Francis I dined with Katherine of Aragon 'with all the honour that was according'.[6] A huge banquet of three courses was served including heron, cygnets, venison, peacock and quail with sweet dishes of fruit, custards and creams to follow each course. Afterwards they were entertained with mummers and dancers. Bryan's sisters Margaret and Elizabeth had accompanied the queen as part of her entourage of ladies and may have also been present. They were however only included as two of the eighteen knight's wives that journeyed with their queen and there were far more nobles ladies in Katherine's entourage including the duchess of Buckingham, seven countesses and sixteen baronesses who took precedence at the banquet.

Henry in turn visited the heavily pregnant French queen Claude taking bands of masquers with him. Bryan, Carew and the Earl of Devonshire were with seven others dressed as Eastlanders in 'doublets guarded with gold, cloaks and hats guarded with gold and silver of damask, hosen and shoes of cloth of gold, purses and girdles of seal skin; their horses trapped with white and yellow damask'[7] for their part in the masque. The Venetian ambassador reported that Henry returned to his Palace of Illusions with his men still dressed '10 in long gowns of cloth of gold, 10 in the Greek costume, violet velvet lined with vair, and 10 in the Swiss fashion, with their plumes and short garments, but slashed with silk and brocade'.[8] The entertainments were lavish and exciting but very nearly turned into disaster.

When Henry and Francis had a wrestling match, the French king outmanoeuvred him with a 'Breton trip' and Henry was thrown to the ground. You can imagine the gasps. Henry called for a rematch but Francis jovially decided it was time for dinner, clapping the English king on the back. Wolsey must have been quivering in his boots and Henry absolutely infuriated. Their meeting was nearly over there and then. Somehow Henry managed to keep his temper and on 24 June took his formal leave of Francis with an exchange of gifts. The whole thing had cost both king's much more than they cared to afford. It has been estimated that Francis spent £40,000 but recouped £13,000 from selling off the tents, fabric, wood, etc whereas Henry spent in the region of £36,000. The Field of the Cloth of Gold had cost £63,000 in Tudor coin, roughly £32 million in today's money.

After weeks of excitement, Bryan accompanied his king and queen along with Nicholas Carew, Henry Guildford and Sir William Fitzwilliam on a more serious matter to meet Charles V and his aunt Margaret of Savoy (once Katherine of Aragon's sister-in-law) at Gravelines on his way home. With Francis I appeased it was time for Henry to cement his relationship with the Holy Roman Emperor. Both Henry and Francis had once coveted the title but Charles, nearly nine years younger than Henry, had succeeded his grandfather, Maximilian, in 1519 and was fast becoming a super power to be reckoned with. Henry may have met with Francis and showed his commitment to the Treaty of London but he was ever wary of the French. It would be as well to have Charles V's support and offer his in return.

Bryan returned to England around 20 July but in August he was required, along with his brother-in-law Henry Guildford, to accompany Wolsey to France and on to Bruges to meet with

Charles V as hostilities increased between the Holy Roman Emperor and Francis I along the French borders and in Italy. As much as Henry would always be eager for war with France, Wolsey was all for peace. He at least knew that if England were to be drawn into war they needed time to prepare and his mission was to talk to both parties to try and negotiate between them. They first met with ambassadors in Calais before they continued on to Bruges. In a report from the Venetian ambassador it appears Bryan arrived first with messages from Wolsey explaining his delay and on 21 August:

> *Master Bryan has apologized to the French ambassadors on behalf of the Cardinal, saying that he had not failed doing his utmost to effect the conclusion, and was to depart on the 22nd for the purpose of returning to Calais with the Imperial ambassadors. The French ambassadors made answer to the Cardinal that they would wait for him. Bryan returns post to Bruges. He made his statement in the presence of the Treasurer of Calais. They then pressed Bryan to breakfast with them, in order to ascertain whether he had anything else to tell. Bryan said he had no farther communication to make.*

This was all done to appease the French ambassadors and the reports from Venice, allied with the French, show they had no indication of what was to happen even though they tried to press Bryan for more information. Bryan took the middle ground trying to appease both sides. He was building a strong relationship with Francis I and his ambassadors but serving his king was paramount.

Wolsey would in fact sign the secret Treaty of Bruges with Charles V. In it Henry agreed to make war on France if they did not cease hostilities with Charles within a limited time. To that end Henry would invade Calais in 1523 with 40,000 men whilst Charles V attacked from Spain. Henry agreed to keep the Channel open for Charles' ships whilst the Holy Roman Emperor agreed to make up for Henry's lost French pension and to marry the princess Mary. 'This treaty to be kept secret from all, except the secret councillors of the contracting parties. When the Pope has ratified these articles, the Emperor and England to do the same'.[10] Charles V also promised to help Wolsey with his bid for the papacy as Henry's Lord Chancellor strove for more power.

The men travelled back to Calais where the cardinal received a letter from his secretary Richard Pace that Henry was anxious to have Bryan and his brother-in-law back in England.

The King has very few to attend on him in his Privy Chambers as he has licensed Sir Wm. Kingston to go to his country, and Sir Wm. Tyler is sick. He wishes you therefore to send home Sir Henry Guylforde and Frauncese Brian, with letters of occurrences there, or other errands as ye think meet.[11]

There was a dearth of young men at court and Henry was missing their company. The king certainly appreciated Bryan as in 1521 as he was made constable of Harlech Castle in Wales, received a grant of all the tenements in the parish of St John the Baptist-super-Walbroke, London and was made steward of the lordship of Flampstead, Hertfordshire and the lordships of Newhall, Boreham, Walkefare and Powers, Essex, with 100s a year. He was also to be master of the hunt in Newhall Park. Bryan was doing very well for himself.

On 29 May 1522 so soon after the camaraderie of the Field of Cloth of Gold, Henry declared war on France and sent his herald to Francis I at Lyons to inform the French king to 'beware of him, as he was his mortal enemy, on account of his infraction of the treaty of Ardre'[12] and then listed Francis' faults including making war on the Emperor, allowing the Duke of Albany to go to Scotland (to become regent in place of Henry's sister Margaret), employing foreigners, invading Navarre and discontinuing his pensions and causing the French to pillage his ships.

The French king replied to his list 'The duke of Albany

left without his knowledge, and he has tried without success to make him return. There was nothing about Navarre in the treaty of Ardre, but the king of England promised to put the said kingdom into his hands in three months, which he has not done. As to the pension, he has felt assured for two years that the King is his mortal enemy, and he will not pay him money to be used against himself. In proof of this assertion he offers to show articles, signed by Henry, and sent by him to the late Pope. Finally, he said he would give the lie to any man who said he had not kept the promise he made at Ardres; if this was Henry's only complaint, it was a bad one, and whenever he chose to come into the field he would be beforehand with him'.[13]

You can imagine Henry's anger when he heard Francis' reply and it would only goad him further to attack the French who he saw as his lifelong enemies regardless of any treaties.

Thomas Howard, now Lord Admiral, was commanded to attack Brittany with a fleet of thirty ships. Bryan was given command of one vessel and accompanied his uncle as they raided villages along the coast culminating in an attack on a French town.

The king said he had received word that on July 1st the admiral, with all his fleet, had arrived in Brittany near a town called Morlaix. He had at once landed the infantry and taken the town by storm, without previous bombardment, in spite of a stout resistance. At the end of three hours the town had been sacked and burned. The English reckon their booty at about 2,000 angels, but the damage done the French at 500,000 crowns, for they burnt fourteen ships, some of a hundred and fifty tons and some larger, besides a great number of small ones. The following day the admiral remained in camp near Morlaix because of a rumour that M. de Laval was coming to fight him. The following day he re-embarked his troops, without seeing the French, but as soon as they were aboard some two hundred French men-at-arms came down as far as the seashore.

This is their customary bragging fashion. The admiral set sail to
see if he could perform a similar exploit at Brest or some other port.

Although Surrey reported that they had encountered severe resistance, the French maintained that the city was defenceless due to the nearby festivities in the town of Noyal which many of the men of Morlaix attended and the absence of the town's soldiers being at a review in Guingamp. There were only a handful of people to resist the English troops. One priest, armed by an arquebus, shot at them from the church tower killing five or six English men and a housemaid covered over a large reservoir of water which several men fell through to their deaths. When local villagers realised Morlaix was under attack they felled several trees in the forest and threw them in the river to try to stop the English ships from leaving with their booty but to no avail.

Again according to French reports 600–700 English men were killed the day after the attack, too drunk from a night of celebrating, to defend themselves against Lieutenant Guy de Laval and his troops. So local legend tells, the 'Feunteun ar Saozon' (fountain of the Saxons) ran red with their blood.

It had been a brutal and bloody foray. Bryan had been in the thick of the action, serving under Sir Richard Wingfield, with a company of 75 men who had been instrumental in taking the town gate. He was knighted for his actions on 1 July 1522 on the beach outside Morlaix by Thomas Howard, Earl of Surrey, later 3rd Duke of Norfolk who 'called to him certain Squires, whom for their hardiness and noble courage he made Knights'.[14] After revictualling at Calais they sailed again to continue their attack along the Brittany coast. They stopped at St Pol-de-Léon one night and Bryan and his men approached the shore in rowboats before destroying many ships anchored in the harbour.

English ambassadors wrote to Margaret of Savoy, regent of the Netherlands, who was pro-English and always eager for information of their ongoing plans:

...the admiral has burned two other Breton villages, St. Pol and Couquet. The cardinal has been busy in the last three days preparing the enterprise which is to commence August first. He asks us to tell you that there will be no default in the artillery, munitions, and troops which his master is supposed to send, or in the money for their payment. He begs you therefore, to have draft horses ready for the artillery, and wagons for the munitions, and provisions, and to have ready money enough to pay for half the horses and wagons. Two hundred and fifty men-at-arms and a thousand horse should also be ready to join the English and our German infantry according to the treaty. He also asks you to have ready a large number of peasant infantry to reinforce the army if the need arises, for he is advised that Francis has abandoned Italy for this year, and intends to concentrate his whole power, 30,000 infantry and all his gens d'armes on the frontier of Flanders near Calais between Ardres and Guines, to guard his frontier, especially Boulogne, Montreuil and the other Channel towns and, if possible, to attack lower Flanders or the Calais pale. To check the French, Wolsey is getting ready 30,000 English infantry, who will be held here in readiness to cross to Calais and give battle to the king of France, if need arises.[15]

The sea raids ceased in July as Henry prepared for a land invasion and Thomas Howard and Bryan were recalled. But there was no rest for either of them. Howard was waiting at Southampton as men and supplies boarded ships to launch another French invasion. Bryan was sent post haste to join him with other young gentlemen.

The Earl of Surrey was charged with taking 15,000 men through France to Paris to join with Charles V's troops. Bryan was amongst the men who journeyed through Picardy laying waste to the villages, towns and castles they encountered including 'Longyngham, Coolis, Brewnbridge, Burneville, Hamever, Caakis, Daverne, Wast, Samerde, Boys, Huckelers, Prewere, Campaigne, Mounterelle, and many othar townes, castles and villages tyll they cam to Hedyng, and that towne they brenyd and leyd sege to the castle, but wan it not'.[16] Despite Surrey's promise to kill all the men, women and children of Hesdin if they did not surrender.

After their failed attempt to capture the castle, well defended by the Duke of Guise and his men, Surrey received instructions from Wolsey:

> *The King has sent me your letters in answer to those he wrote to you by Sir Francis Brian, and desired me to answer you. You wish to know the King's pleasure, whether to save next month's wages by returning in case you cannot find an opportunity of doing any notable act, and also what you shall do if the Emperor's army wish you to go to Terouenne. I wrote to you lately, advising you, for many reasons, to remain till the approach of winter, and informed the King of what I had advised you by sending him a copy of my letter, and by another letter written to Sir Thos. More, a copy of which, and of his answer made to me by the King's command, I enclose. It is his pleasure, therefore, now that the Emperor's army is so thoroughly united with you, and that Flanders is so well disposed to supply you with victuals, that you remain, not only during this month of September, but also during October, unless you receive orders to the contrary, march into the Boulonnois, and burn and destroy fortresses, taking care to do everything with the consent of the Emperor's army, so as to avoid all jealousies.*[17]

But by the end of September Surrey was asking to disband the army. Sickness was rife amongst the men with nine English men dying as well as forty-seven 'Almains, Spaniards and Burgundians'.[18] He reported that he could not blame his men for being afraid as 'for he that is whole and merry at noon is dead by midnight, and when they be dead their bodies as black as a coal.'[19] The men were ordered to turn back for Calais burning and destroying towns on their way.

Bryan had proved himself a soldier that year but was back in

England by early November when he was appointed as sheriff for Hertfordshire and Essex. Bryan had at some point turned to thoughts of married life and by 1522 he was wed to Philippa, daughter and heir of Humphrey Spice and widow of John Fortescue of Ponsbourne in Hertfordshire. Philippa was born around 1484, making her somewhat older than Bryan, and had married Fortescue around 1510 when she

> brought to her husband a very great state although she did not inherit her father's state of Black Notley. Through her, Falkborne Hall came to her husband, and became the principal residence of this family.[20]

Faulkbourne became their family home and Bryan could escape from court to this red brick turreted manor house in Essex when he was not serving the king. Little is known of Philippa. She does not appear to have been at court and so may have been introduced to Bryan through family connections. She had had one son from her marriage to John Fortescue and Bryan was granted the wardship of his stepson Henry in March 1522. This wardship he subsequently sold on 'for [a] great sum of money'[21] to Sir Andrew Windsor, a seasoned soldier and Keeper of the Great Wardrobe. Henry, who would later inherit Faulkbourne Hall, was severely unhappy with his new guardian. Windsor kept him away from his mother but as he approached his majority Henry was eventually allowed to see her and during a visit he escaped Windsor's house in Stanwell. Windsor would go on to sue Bryan, his wife and stepson in an effort to recoup his loss. He would not be the first enemy Bryan made.

The Field of the Cloth of Gold

Chapter Three

A Soldier in Scotland

1523–1526

The ongoing war with France led to difficulties with Scotland, both countries being sworn together as allies through their 'Auld Alliance' dating back to 1295. Henry's sister Margaret had once held the regency after the death of James IV but the Scottish Council had replaced her with the Duke of Albany, a descendant of James II, who now had orders from King Francis I to invade England. The duke mustered a force of 80,000 men to advance towards the Scottish border where Henry's men were raiding towns like Kelso, Eccles, Ednam and Stichell.

The duke wanted to march on Carlisle but he did not have the support of the Scottish nobles who felt they were being used for France's aims. They told him, 'We, noble earls and lords, are here convened at our Governor's authority, obedient to his will: but we come to defend our own, not to conquer our neighbours. Although at this time we are bent to hold the Englishmen from our boundaries if they attack, with all our force as we are bound to do, nevertheless we are neither able to set on them within their boundaries, nor will it be to the profit of our people or commodity of our country'.[1] Albany replied with a rousing speech but after the terrible defeat of the Scots at Flodden in 1513, when Margaret's husband James IV and around 10,000 men were killed, the Scottish lords would not endanger themselves and their men by fighting for the French. Many of the nobility had been slain and generations of young men wiped out. Instead of the invasion he had planned the duke was forced to sign a truce in September and the following month was recalled to France to answer to Francis for his lack of military action.

Henry saw a chance to see his sister rise again to power and commanded Sir William Fitzwilliam to watch the channel with a 'fleet of strong and tall ships'[2] to stop the duke from leaving France and returning to Scotland. Boulogne was blockaded but Wolsey had intelligence that Albany was staying in the coastal town of Le Tréport, northeast of Dieppe. The recently knighted Sir Francis Bryan had command of one ship and whilst some vessels remained at Boulogne, Fitzwilliam, Bryan and a few others sailed for Le Tréport.

Hall recalls in his chronicle that as soon as the French saw them nearing they fired their beacons and strengthened and manned the town. The English came ashore at seven in the morning under fire from the French bulwarks and their ships returned the barrage. As the French ran for the safety of the town walls, the English fired arrows at them and 'then the captains cried Saint George, to the gates of Tréport'.[3] One man had found a section of mast that was used as a battering ram but under continual fire, they were unable to break through the gate. Retreating the English burnt whatever they came across including seven ships and were almost back to their boats when the number of Frenchmen swelled and 'found on land Francis Newdigate, Thomas Wagham, Serjeant Rotte and other captains to the number of twelve and ran hastily towards them in great number'.[4] Fitzwilliam shot at the French from his ship and saved the lives of his men. Albany was nowhere to be seen and in fact was departing from Brest much further down the coast while the English were otherwise occupied. For all of Henry's efforts to stop the duke reaching Scotland, he was back at Kirkcudbright on 21 September with 4000 French soldiers and new artillery including twenty-eight cannon and six hundred horse.

Whilst trouble was brewing in Scotland, a land invasion under Charles Brandon, the Duke of Suffolk was underway in France. By September Boulogne was under siege but Henry wanted his 10,000 troops to take Paris and Brandon received orders to push on. He reached Compiegne, fifty miles outside of Paris, with a lack of reinforcements. His troops were suffering with the cold, one hundred dying of frostbite in two days and so Brandon ordered their retreat. Henry was torn between France and Scotland and neither campaign was bringing him the glory and victory he wanted.

The Earl of Surrey was in charge of the army now moving north towards Scotland. Bryan, Carew and others were sent to him with reinforcements. He hoped for their arrival around the 17th October and they had definitely arrived by the 23rd. There was some cause for celebration when Surrey's report of 3 November told of Albany's failed attempt to take Wark Castle on the 1st.

At 3 p.m. on Monday, the Tweed being too high to ford, Albany sent 2,000 Frenchmen in boats to assault the place. They entered the basecourt, and were kept back for an hour and a half by Sir Wm. Lizle, captain of the castle, and 100 men. At length they gained the inner ward, but were immediately attacked by Lizle, and driven out of both the inner and outer wards, and ten persons slain. Received notice, at 3 this morning, from Lizle, that he could not keep the place without help, and advanced to his rescue at break of day; but Albany, hearing of it, retreated with his whole force.[5]

With Albany's withdrawal Surrey's men were sent to patrol the border. Bryan patrolled between Coldstream and Berwick whilst they waited to hear if Albany would return. The army was unable to stand down until they knew the threat of war was over. But winter was approaching and Surrey was desperate to return home. He requested his recall at least three times until they received news that the duke had ceased hostilities. Surrey pleaded that 'Sir Nich. Carew, Sir Francis Bryan and others here can testify to the state he is in' and again 'Sir Nich. Carewe and Sir Francis Brian can bear witness that 'the little flesh I had is clean gone; and yet I am not sick, but in manner I eat very little, and these five weeks day I never slept one whole hour without waking ... But I know myself to be as a washing horse is that will lose flesh and soon recover it again'[6] and by the end of November they were all returning home.

Bryan was given the stewardship of Hanslope, Castelthorpe and Cosgrave in Buckinghamshire on 20 June 1523 and in December, along with Sir William Compton, he was awarded joint constable of Warwick Castle as well as 'keeper of the manor of Goodrest, with garden and waters, in Weggenok park, Warw., parker of the said park and master of the hunt therein; with herbage and pannage, and the fishery in the said park ... and fees out of the manors of Warwyk, Snytterfeld, Kyngton, Barkeswell, Moreton, Lyghtern, Weggenok, Claredon and Henley-Arderns'[7] but even with more benefices he ended the year owing £333 6s 8d to the treasury. War was a costly business both for the crown and those who served it.

In May 1524, Sir William Fitzwilliam, was made governor of Guînes, a position of strategic importance being on the border of the Pale of Calais. Carew, who had spent some time as Lieutenant of Calais, and Bryan were mentioned as being in France in his dispatch to Wolsey.

On his departure Bry[on] sent his recommendations to me, Carew and Bryan, saying he was sorry the world was of that sort that we could not be merry together, for no one desired peace more than the king of France.[8]

What they were doing back in France is not clear. Wolsey could see that England could not afford another French war and to this end he was conducting secret peace negotiations with the French. Philippe de Chabot, seigneur de Brion, mentioned in Fitzwilliam's correspondence, had grown up with Francis I and would later be Admiral of France and the French ambassador to England. Were they discussing how to avert further hostilities? Carew and Bryan both had experience of the French court and were trusted advisors. Perhaps Wolsey had instructed them to act on his behalf.

Henry was certainly still happy to involve himself in French hostilities and the king may have been unaware of what Bryan and Carew were doing. In June Henry sent his ambassadors, Pace and Russell, to Charles, the Duke of Bourbon to support the siege of Marseilles and sent £20,000 for his campaign. The duke had once been constable of France but after continuing disagreements with Francis I, he offered his services to the Holy Roman Emperor. At the head of an 11,000 strong Imperial army Bourbon crossed the Alps to Provence sacking and destroying French villages. He made his way to Marseilles but there was routed by Francis I's troops. Henry had backed yet another disastrous campaign.

Bryan did not stay away in France for long. He was needed back at court and was elected as a commissioner to collect subsidies in Essex in 1524 and was a commissioner of the peace for Buckinghamshire early the next year. He continued with his local responsibilities and Christmas saw him attending court for the joust.

A fabulous mock castle was built in the tilt yard at Greenwich – the Castle of Loyalty – that the king had given to four maidens and was protected by fifteen defenders. As the defenders arrived at the castle, there was a disturbance, two ladies led out two ancient knights, dressed in purple damask, their hair and beards flowing with silver. They were taken to Queen Katherine who was asked to give permission for these old men to compete in the jousts. Once Katherine agreed, they threw back their robes and ripped off their wigs and beards to reveal the king and the Duke of Suffolk, who continued to battle the defenders to the thrill of the crowd.

Bryan and Thomas Wyatt, the poet and fellow ambassador, were amongst the defenders. It is possible they had met previously at court but this would be the first time they worked together to please the king and would certainly not be the last. Their relationship would become much closer in the coming years.

In January 1525 Bryan was sent to take an inventory of stores at the king's beerhouses in Portsmouth with Arthur Plantagenet, Lord Lisle, the illegitimate son of Edward IV, whom Bryan would also have a lasting friendship. A new beerhouse had been built in Portsmouth in April 1513 to cope with the increasing amounts of beer needed by the army to the tune of 500 barrels a day. Leyland recorded in his itinerary that Henry's father 'King Henry the vij. at his firste warres into Fraunce erectid in the south part of the towne 3. great bruing houses with the implementes to serve his shippes at such tyme as they shaul go to the se in tyme of warre.'[9] These were expanded and equipped to continue provision during Henry VIII's reign.

Henry had not given up his policy against France but whilst England stayed out of Charles V and Francis I's conflicts in 1525, February saw the capture of the French king at the Battle of Pavia. It was a humiliating defeat for Francis with 10,000 soldiers losing their lives. Henry saw an opportunity to seize the French crown for himself but with the failure of the amicable grant to raise funds (a tax that Wolsey had hoped would raise £800,000), no support from the Holy Roman Emperor who now wanted peace, and the Lord Chancellor counselling against another French campaign, the king's plans came to nothing.

The mother of the King of France, Louise of Savoy, acted as regent whilst her son was in captivity and was instrumental in negotiating peace with England. The Duke of Suffolk once described her as 'she who runs all, and so may she well; for I never saw a woman like to her, both for wit, honour and dignity. She hath a great stroke in all matters with the King her son'.[10] As Francis I was imprisoned at Pavia, then Genoa, Naples, Barcelona and Madrid she assured him 'I shall support the misfortune in such a manner for the succour of your little children and the affairs of your kingdom that I shall not give you occasion for more pain'.[11]

Henry, so furious with Charles V for not backing his bid to take France for himself, agreed to a truce. The Treaty of the More, negotiated by Wolsey, was signed on 30 August 1525 between England and France. Henry agreed to give up his claims to French territory and agreed to help secure Francis' release whilst France would pay him a pension of £20,000 a year and what was due to Henry's sister Mary as dowager queen of France. For once Henry would be at peace with his enemies – at least for the next eighteen years.

Wolsey may have brokered peace but he was ever aware of his control at court slipping. In his Eltham Ordinance of 1526 suddenly Bryan as well as Nicholas Carew, William Compton and George Boleyn found themselves pushed out of the privy chamber and close proximity to Henry. Sir William Taylor, Sir Thomas Cheney, Sir Anthony Browne, Sir John Russell, Henry Norris and William Carey were now to be the gentlemen of the privy chamber, reducing Henry's household from twelve men to six. Their instructions were clear.

> The persons of the privy chamber to be friendly to each other, and keep secret all things done there; not to inquire in the King's absence where he is going, or talk about his pastimes; and if any one uses any unfitting language of the King, it is to be immediately reported … None of the chamber to advance himself further in service than he is appointed by the King, nor to press him with suits except when commanded, but the nearer they are to his person the more humble they must show themselves.[12]

It was a cost-saving measure and one that Henry agreed to – at the time. It wouldn't be long before he missed his old familiars. Henry's minions were still accounted for in a list of 'Persons assigned to have lodging in the King's house when they repair to it' but Wolsey made it quite plain they were not welcome and had had an undue influence on the king.

Bryan still had his work at court although it has been suggested that he and the other previous privy gentlemen were banished for a time. He is now mentioned as master of the henchmen, to look after Henry's pages or young boys from noble families, for the first time. This position was first recorded in the 1340s and by 1471 the description of the role of master of the henchmen was

> ...to learn them to ride cleanly and surely, to draw them also to jousts, to learn them wear their harness (armour), to have all courtesy in words, deeds, and degrees... to teach them sundry languages and other learnings virtuous, to harping, to pipe, sing, dance, and with other honest and temperate behaving and patience... to have his respects unto their demeaning, how mannerly they eat and drink, and to their communication.[13]

It is uncertain how much the role had changed by Bryan's time but he still had his duties to attend to although he was also involved in family problems. His wife Philippa was in chancery court for debts occurring before their marriage in January 1526. One Jasper Fyloll, a gentleman usher, was trying to recover £171 which was now Bryan's responsibility. Philippa's first husband John Fortescue had paid Fyloll an annual fee of 40s with the right to live in their house at Faulkbourne, but Fortescue had died in arrears with the fee. Fyloll had helped Philippa in her widowhood but Bryan had him unceremoniously removed from the house without paying him what he was owed. Whether the court ruled Bryan had to make good on the debt is not known.

Bryan was back at Greenwich for the Shrove Tuesday joust which would be momentous for two reasons. Hall recorded how well the combatants were dressed 'the Marques and his bend wer in Grene Veliiet, & crimosyn sattyn embrodered with hartes burnyng, and ouer euery harte a Ladies hand commyng out of acloude, holdyng a garden water pot, which dropped siluer droppes on the harte'.[14] But more stunning was what the king was wearing. He was dressed in richly embroidered cloth of gold and silver with a man's heart in a press with flames about it and in letters were written, 'Declare ie nose, in Englishe, Declare I dare not'. The theme of the joust was unrequited love and the king's motto signalled his growing attraction to Bryan's cousin, Anne Boleyn.

Anne was the daughter of Thomas Boleyn and Elizabeth Howard, Lady Bryan's half-sister. Born at Blickling Hall and educated in France, she had returned home to become one of the queen's ladies-in-waiting. She had almost married James Butler, the 9th Earl of Ormond and had been betrothed to Henry Percy, later Earl of Northumberland, but both relationships were quashed. Her older sister Mary had once been the king's mistress but it was Anne who had now caught his eye.

Thomas Wyatt's grandson George wrote of how his grandfather had been enamoured of Anne from the moment of her return to court. Although the accuracy of his stories have been debated he wrote of how Wyatt 'caught from her a certain small jewel hanging by a lace out of her pocket, which he thrust into his bosom'. Later on when the king was playing bowls with Bryan he declared he was winning although Wyatt disagreed. 'And yet still (the king) pointing with his finger whereon he ware her ring, replied often it was his, and especially to the Knight he said "Wyat I tell thee it is mine"'. Wyatt replied 'And if it may like your Majestie to give me leave to measure it, I hope it will be mine' as he took from his breast the jewel which he had strung on a lace to wear around his neck. The king seeing Anne's token grumpily kicked at the bowl and said 'It may be so, but then I am deceived'.[15]

Anne was now firmly in the picture as Bryan well knew. Not

yet as a wife for the king but it was becoming plain to all that Henry was enamoured of her. Bryan could not have cared less at the time. As he jousted that day a spear splintered against his visor. He lost his eye but remarkably he survived. He would ever after wear a patch and it was said that because of it he would never let his portrait be painted. Certainly none survive.

Francis I

Chapter Four

A Changing World

1527–1529

The year 1527 would see the start of a process that would change England and its people forever. Henry's lack of male heirs and infatuation with Anne Boleyn propelled him on a journey that would end in England's break with Rome and have devastating consequences for the queen. Henry's infatuation came as no surprise to Katherine. She had not lived with her husband as man and wife since 1524 and it was plain for all to see that he was pursuing another but never in her wildest dreams did she think the king would put her aside. She had the might of the Church behind her and support of the Holy Roman Emperor, Charles V, her nephew.

But Rome was in disarray. Charles had defeated the French army in Italy but his troops commanded by the Duke of Bourbon mutinied over lack of pay and continued on to Rome. Arriving at the beginning of May they killed thousands of the inhabitants and looted and pillaged the city causing utter chaos and destruction. Pope Clement VII was imprisoned and would remain incarcerated for six months.

In England while news of this barbarity slowly filtered in, Wolsey was spearheading covert hearings to discuss Henry's dilemma, culminating in a convocation held on 31 May. His discussions may have been kept secret from Katherine but she was soon to find out. The Spanish ambassador reported that Henry had 'secretly assembled certain bishops and lawyers that they may sign a declaration to the effect that his marriage with the Queen is null and void on account of her being his brother's wife'.[1]

Henry was asked to appear as a defendant to answer why he had been living in sin with Arthur's widow. It was a staged event. But the ecclesiastical deliberations came to nothing as the situation in Europe became more pressing and Wolsey ruled the matter needed more consultation with theologians and lawyers. They could not consult with Rome as the pope was imprisoned. If Henry had hoped for an easy victory it was plain now that his way forward would not be so simple.

Henry told the queen in June that he was seeking a divorce. He should never have married his brother's wife and in the eyes of God it was a sin. He told Katherine his conscience troubled him and it might be best if she retire. The queen could not believe what she was hearing, refusing to agree, and 'she desired to have counsel as well of strangers as of English, — a device which never could have come into her head except it had been suggested; and therefore Wolsey suggested that the King should handle her gently, until it was shown what the Pope and Francis would do'.[2] This was not just going to be a case solved easily in England but would have international ramifications in which Sir Francis Bryan would play his part.

In July 1527 Bryan accompanied Wolsey on his journey to meet with Francis I, who had been released from captivity in Spain in March 1526.

Then marched he forward out of his own house at Westminster, passing through all London, over London Bridge, having before him of gentlemen a great number, three in a rank, in black velvet livery coats, and the most part of them with great chains of gold about their necks, and all his yeomen, with noblemen's and gentlemen's servants following him in French tawny livery coats; having embroidered upon the backs and breasts of the said coats these letters: T. and C., under the cardinal's hat. His sumpter mules, which were twenty in number and more, with his carts and other carriages of his train, were passed on before, conducted and guarded with a great number of bows and spears. He rode like a cardinal, very sumptuously, on a mule trapped with crimson velvet upon velvet, and his stirrups of copper and gilt; and his spare mule following him with like apparel. And before him he had his two great crosses of silver, two great pillars of silver, the great seal of England, his cardinal's hat, and a gentleman that carried his valaunce, otherwise called a cloakbag; which was made altogether of fine scarlet cloth, embroidered over and over with cloth of gold very richly, having in it a cloak of fine scarlet. Thus passed he through London, and all the way of his journey, having his harbingers passing before to provide lodgings for his train.[3]

The cardinal left London with 900 horse and stopped at Sir John Wiltshire's house in Dartford, was entertained by Henry Guildford and his half-brother Edward at Rochester, stayed at the abbey at Faversham and met up with the abbot of St Austin's at Canterbury. At each place he stopped Wolsey tried to find out what rumours had spread before him and what they knew of the king's secret matter.

Bryan's brother-in-law Guildford was sent on to Calais to make arrangements for the cardinal's arrival. He had recently helped Thomas Wyatt in arranging for a new banqueting hall to be built at Greenwich. His role of Master of the Horse was passed on to Nicholas Carew and he became the king's comptroller, also receiving a pension from Francis I. Guildford, widowed around this time, would later fall foul of Anne Boleyn's temper.

By 11 July Wolsey and his entourage had arrived at Calais to find it in disrepair and its soldiers unpaid. It was not their concern and they hurriedly journeyed into France to meet with the French king. The peace treaty of Westminster had been signed in April between England and France and it included the Princess Mary's marriage to Francis' son Henri of Orléans. Wolsey was to discuss further the arrangements with the French king and decide what to do about Charles V as well as attend a meeting with other cardinals in Avignon to consult on papal affairs. Behind it all was the quest for support for Henry's divorce.

Wolsey, Bryan and their entourage travelled to Montreuil and Abbeville. Wolsey was anxious to meet with Francis who had agreed to meet him at Amiens but was delayed due to ill health in his family. Wolsey wrote to Henry 'He will not allow me to repair to him elsewhere, much to my discomfort'.[4] Finally Wolsey met the French king at the beginning of August and told him:

> That, though unworthy, I had been appointed your lieutenant, chiefly to settle three things: the marriage of my lady Princess, deliverance of his children, and of the Pope. He expressed himself extremely anxious for his marriage with the Princess. And I asked him, as being her god-father, if it should take effect, how a peace would be made between him and the Emperor, and how his children would be delivered. To this he could give no reply. I then pointed out to him that much as he and you might desire the marriage, both of you must give up your wishes in order that he might recover his children. He then professed to be willing to treat on his own marriage with lady Eleanor, and that of the duke of Orleans with the Princess.[5]

Charles held Francis' two sons captive, surety for his release after the Battle of Pavia and Henry had promised to help see them returned. Wolsey had important matters to discuss but he wrote to Henry that he had not yet spoken of his divorce and would not until all other matters were settled. Then when the treaty was signed he informed the king 'Nothing now remains except to disclose your private matter, which I propose to do in so cloudy and dark a sort that he shall not know your utter determination'.[6]

And Henry was determined. That summer saw him writing love letters to Anne, expressing his desire for her. When Bryan and Wolsey returned in the autumn, they were both to find that Anne had become more of a fixture at court and was never far from the king's side.

When Wolsey hurried to the king to give him his personal report on his dealings in France Anne was with Henry.

At the end of September the Legate returned from France with all those who had accompanied him on that journey, and immediately after repaired to Richmond, where the King was then staying. On his arrival at that royal residence the Legate sent to apprise the King of his return, and ask where and at what hour he could see him, it being the custom that whenever the Legate has state affairs to communicate, the King retires to a private closet with him. Now it happened that on this occasion the lady called Anna de Bolains, who seems to entertain no great affection for the Cardinal, was in the room with the King, and before the latter could answer the message she said, "Where else is the Cardinal to come? Tell him that he may come here, where the King is." This answer being confirmed by the King, the messenger returned, and the Legate, though extremely annoyed at a circumstance which boded no good to him, dissembled as much as he could, and concealed his resentment.[7]

Wolsey would have a world of trouble in front of him over the coming year but Bryan was back at court and in favour, boosted by his cousin's rise in the king's affections. In March of this year the members of the king's household amongst others had their lands assessed in lieu of payment of the subsidy – an early tax initiative. Sir William Compton was the highest of the king's men at £1,100, Lord Lisle £900, Sir William Fitzwilliam £666 and both Bryan and Carew at £400. They were both benefiting from serving the king but although their lands may have been extensive being a courtier was a costly business and they would both find themselves in debt to the crown and others repeatedly.

In November Bryan visited the Abbot of Peterborough. It

is possible that Wolsey had sent him to collect a contribution of 2000 marks that the abbot, Robert Kirton, had promised for Wolsey's new college in Oxford. When Bryan wrote to thank the abbot for his hospitality he was staying in Lincoln. He asked that Kirton should 'send up the Scot in his keeping with some sure man, "honestly to handle him by the way unto the King's highness"'[8] but who this man was is a mystery.

Bryan was so restored that by June 1528 he was back to being a gentleman of the privy chamber. It was a terrible summer with the sweating sickness cutting a swath across the country. Anne Boleyn was at Hever and suffering herself. Henry sent his physician Dr Butts to her and she eventually recovered. Henry was so scared of the sweating sickness he asked Bryan to sleep in his chamber with him. He was right to be scared. William Carey, Mary Boleyn's husband, died of it on 22 June and Bryan himself caught the sickness and was ill for six weeks.

But illness would not put Bryan off for long and in August he was sent to escort Cardinal Lorenzo Campeggio to England. The pope had agreed that the papal legate should travel to England to consult with Wolsey and the king to decide on his divorce situation.

Bryan had a terrible crossing and wrote from Boulogne:

Had never a worse passage. Was ten hours at sea in a boat of six ton. Could not make Calais, as the wind was E.N.E., and ran the boat aground at Sandgate, and were nearly lost. When they landed, at 10 at night, were fain to hire a wagon, and reached Calais at midnight. Delivered Wolsey's letter to the Deputy. Have arranged to set forward the spearmen and horse. Is at Boulogne. Did not find Dew Bees, but his deputy, who brought him to his lodging with many gentlemen. The mayor sent him a present of wine, and offered to put the town under his command. Intends to leave tomorrow at three in the morning. Hopes to be at Paris on Wednesday night or Thursday early. Begs Wolsey will excuse his rude hand, as his secretary has fallen ill.[9]

Bryan reached Paris and had an audience with Francis I. He was asked to attend the coming of a herald from the Emperor and sign as witness a public notarial document on the proposed single combat between the French king and Charles V in September. Both England and France had declared war on Charles V in January and in March Charles challenged Francis to a duel, a challenge he had already made in 1526, which the French king accepted. Francis wanted the emperor's herald to give him security for the battlefield but when it wasn't immediately forthcoming the king was furious and railed at the herald sending him packing with the words:

> *Thy master cannot lay down law in France; and things have come to such a pass that there is no longer need of words, and thou must be aware that I did not send thy master words by herald; but what I announced to him was in writing, signed in my own hand, which needs no other reply than this security for the field; without which I have determined not to give thee audience, as thou mightest say things which would be denied thee; whereas my speech and battle do not concern thee, but solely the Emperor.*[10]

Bryan had to continue with his task and whilst there he met with Campeggio. 'On meeting him he is to thank him for his diligence on behalf of the King and Wolsey, to deliver the King's letters and the mule, and conduct him to Calais, accompanied by the said spears and horsemen'.[11]

Campeggio was suffering with gout and it would make their onward journey slow and arduous but they were at Canterbury by the beginning of October. Bryan wrote to the king:

> *Please it your Grace to be advertised, I [was with the Legate (Campeggio) on] Wednesday, on Barron Downe, to w[elcome him with congratu-]lassions both of the King's behalf [and your*

Grace's,] the which he was very glad of, fur[ther showing him how, seeing] that your Grace understood that he w[as troubled] with the gout, for that ye sent hy[m a litter,] which lytter I presented unto him, [which he graciously received,] thanking the King and your Grace [for your care of him], saying that he was so glad to come [to do the King and your] Grace service, that the remembrance o[f it took] away all his pain. I found him [mounted on a mule], and so rode all the way, and as far ... [I stayed] by him. If the weather be fair he wy[ll continue] on his mule.[12]

Henry let Anne, who had retired to the countryside for appearance's sake, know the cardinal was on his way in a note and added 'then I trust within a while after to enjoy that which I have so long longed for to God's pleasure and our both comfort'.[13] Henry had all his hopes fixed on a speedy solution once Campeggio ruled on his divorce.

But Henry and Anne were to be disappointed. Campeggio was at first too ill to meet the king and then when he did he urged him to seriously consider the sanctity of marriage, much to Henry's dismay, in a bid to find a way to delay the proceedings in the hope the king would change his mind. Pope Clement VII had given him specific instructions to stall for as long as possible although he held a decretal commission that gave himself and Wolsey the power to judge the validity of the king's marriage.

Campeggio commented 'His Majesty has studied this case so diligently that I believe he knows more about it than a great theologian or jurist. He told me briefly that he wished nothing except a declaration whether his marriage was valid or not, always presuming it was not, and I think that an angel descending from heaven could not persuade him otherwise'.[14]

Queen Katherine met the cardinal on 24 October. He was still in pain and had to be carried to her on a red velvet litter. If she had hoped he would support her cause she was sorely disappointed. Instead he suggested she enter a convent but she refused. Now she produced a papal brief given to her mother Isabella of Castile in 1503. Wolsey and Campeggio wrote to the pope 'that the Queen has exhibited a copy of the brief of Julius II., dated at the same time as the bull, but they suspect its genuineness. Besides its unexpected appearance on such an occasion, it seems incredible that such a document should have been obtained'.[15]

The brief allowed for the consummation of her marriage to Arthur and had been issued regardless although Katherine would later take an oath that her marriage to Henry's brother was unconsummated. Even if consummation had taken place, her marriage to Henry was approved by the pope quashing the king's point that to marry his brother's wife was wrong in the eyes of canonical law.

Henry wanted the original copy claiming this could only be a forgery and now sent Bryan and Peter Vannes, one of Wolsey's men, to Rome to treat with the Pope, promote peace between Francis I and Charles V and look for the brief.

At the beginning of December Bryan and Vannes reported: 'After a severe tempest, arrived at Calais at 8 o'clock, after dreadful nausea and vomiting of blood by one of us, whom we do not wish to particularise. Will proceed on their journey without delay'.[16] The journey forward was slow due to bad roads and the lack of light during the winter months. At Chambery they found out that Campeggio had been told to delay the divorce proceedings and duly reported this to Wolsey. From Florence Bryan sent another report and ended with 'I would have written to my mistress that shall be, (Anne Boleyn) but I will not write unto her till I may write that shall please her most in this world. I pray God to send your Grace and her long life and merry, or else me a short end'.[17]

They arrived in Rome 25 January and the next day reported 'We have searched all the registers, and can find no brief. We have written to the cardinal (Wolsey) about it'.[18] They could not yet seek an audience with the pope as he was severely ill to the point his death was mistakenly reported in February. In fact he had written to Campeggio 'Whereas it has come to the Pope's knowledge that the whole controversy of the divorce has turned upon the insufficiency of the dispensation found in the English State Paper office, and that the Queen has exhibited the copy of a brief, of which the original is in Spain, but not found in England, respecting the genuineness of which great doubts are entertained; we authorise you to reject whatever evidence is tendered in behalf of this brief as an evident forgery, and to proceed according to the tenor of our previous letters'.[19] Bryan knew Campeggio was not to be trusted telling Henry 'It is reported here that Campeggio is thoroughly Imperial, and for your matter there could not have been a worse one sent'.[20]

As nothing was happening in England fresh instructions were sent to Bryan and Vannes 'In all their doings they must have regard to the undelayed perfection of the King's great matter, and in no wise consent that it shall remain in suspense upon any treaty'.[21] Henry wanted an answer and he wanted it now but it was still not to be forthcoming.

The French king had heard rumours that Bryan and his colleagues had offered the pope a large sum of money to agree the king's matter and that 'the Imperialists boasted that they would obtain money on this pretext, and that the King would in the end be deluded by the Pope'.[22] Francis wrote to Bryan, a sign of their friendship, to tell him he did not believe Henry would allow him to make such an offer.

They finally met with the pope in March but Bryan had nothing good to report for 'it might well be in his paternoster, but it was nothing in his creed'.[23] A growing sense of frustration creeps into Bryan's correspondence and by April he was reporting:

You sent me here to instruct you how matters proceed. Master Stevyns (Gardiner), Gregory (de Casale), Peter (Vannes) and I have done what we could. You will see by "your farmer letter" (our former letter) to the Cardinal that the Pope will do nothing for you; and were I to write otherwise, I should put you in hope, where none is; and whoever has told you that he will, has not done you, I think, the best service. There is no man more sorry to write this news than I am. No men are more heavy than we are, that we cannot bring things to pass as we would. I trust never to die but that your Grace will be able to requite the Pope and "Popys," and not be fed with their flattering words. I have written to my cousin Anne; but I dare not write to her the truth, but will refer her to your Grace, to make her privy to all the news.[24]

Bryan points to Wolsey in this letter or perhaps Campeggio as not doing the king his best service. And he had nothing better to say in his next letter.

Since my last of the 21st, we have, according to your commandment by Alysaunder, opened all to the Pope, first by fair means and then by foul; but neither fair nor foul will serve, as you will see by our letter to the Cardinal. You will see by our common letters, a copy of which we send, in what situation we are. Master Stevens, in the presence of the Pope, so answered for your Grace that he made the Pope ashamed of his own deeds, who would have excused the cause as best he could. As for what you write to us, that Campeggio is your servant, and will do what he can for you, these are fair words only because he wishes to have the bishopric of Durham. He has written here to the Pope to say that neither he nor Francis Campanys ever made any special promise to your Grace, but in general words, and he bids the Pope trust to it, as the Pope might be sure of him. What- ever they tell you the Pope will do for you is "the glose and not the text." This is true, for the Pope showed the letter to Master Stevens and Master Peter (Vannes). If the Cardinal feels aggrieved, or any other, let him kick; for I do it not of malice, but according to my duty. I could tell you more of my mind in an hour's

talking than I could write in a week, and shall be glad to come home,
as I can do you here no service. "I dare not write unto my cousin
Anne the truth of this matter, because I do not know your Grace's
pleasure whether I shall so do or no; wherefore, if she be angry with
me, I most humbly desire your Grace to make mine excuse.[25]

In May Wolsey instructed Bryan and Gardiner to return. Rumours
were circling that Bryan had slept with a courtesan to gain
intelligence in Rome adding to his reputation as a womaniser.

She lying a night with Sir Francis Bryan
disclosed to him the whole matter
which when he perceived the cardinal's treason
thought to procure her the letter to obtain.[26]

But however he had found out his information there was no
more to be done. The Venetian ambassador reported that Bryan
left dissatisfied with Rome but that he was to visit Venice on his
return and as he 'is much in favour with his king, so it would be
advisable to give him good greeting'.[27]

In England Wolsey and Campeggio would open official
proceedings at the Legatine court at Blackfriars 31 May 1529 to
put forward twelve articles against the king's marriage. Henry
hoped this would finalise his divorce but he had doubts and was
also suspicious of Campeggio after Bryan's intelligence. He sent
Charles Brandon, the duke of Suffolk over to the king of France
to find out more. Suffolk reported:

I told him that you had been advertised by Bryan "that he should
say unto the said Bryan, how do the King my brother's affairs
concerning the divorce? and the said Bryan should say, I trust well.
Upon the which he should say, Well, there be some which the King
my brother doth trust in that matter that would it should never
take effect... He admits these words; says they were spoken upon

communication with Campeggio, who told Francis he was going to England and afterwards to Spain by commission of the Pope. On which Francis asked him how he could go into Spain, and yet do what the king of England wished for the divorce; and he replied that he did not think that the divorce would take effect, but should be dissembled well enough.[28]

He also enquired of Francis how he found Wolsey:

What say you of the cardinal of England in this matter? and he replied, When he was with me, as far as I could perceive, he desired that the divorce might take place, for he loved not the Queen; but I advise my good brother not to put too much trust in any man, whereby he may be deceived, and the best remedy is to look to his own matters himself; —saying further that the cardinal of England had great intelligence with the Pope and with Campeggio, and, as they are not inclined to the divorce, it is the more needful for the King to have regard to his own affairs.[29]

Bryan himself was to meet with Francis on his way back to England but meanwhile the proceedings had started. Katherine lodged an appeal with Rome against Wolsey and Campeggio's authority to try the matter in England and she was determined to fight every step of the way. She gave an emotional speech on 21 June, on her knees in front of her husband, but Henry was unmoved by anything she had to say.

At the end of July Campeggio adjourned the court until October as he said he had to consult with the pope. Henry was infuriated. Katherine's appeal was accepted and so there would be no ruling on his divorce any time soon. Bryan was not there to hear Campeggio's closing speech. So soon after he returned home, he had already been sent back to France.

Henry wrote to the pope in September from Windsor:

On the return to your Holiness of cardinal Campeggio, we could have wished, not less for your sake than our own, that all things had been so expedited as to have corresponded to our expectations, not rashly conceived, but owing to your promises. As it is, we are compelled to regard with grief and wonder the incredible confusion which has arisen. If the Pope can relax Divine laws at his pleasure, surely he has as much power over human laws. Complains that he has often been deceived by the Pope's promises, on which there is no dependence to be placed; and that his dignity has not been consulted in the treatment he has received. If the Pope, as his ambassadors write, will perform what he has promised, and keep the cause now advoked to Rome in his own hands, until it can be decided by impartial judges, and in an indifferent place, in a manner satisfactory to the King's scruples, he will forget what is past, and repay kindness by kindness, as Campeggio will explain.[30]

But the pope would not give him what he wanted. He thought that his marriage to Katherine was valid and the dispensation had been 'perfectly sound'.[31]

Campeggio took his leave of Henry in September at Grafton. He was accompanied by Wolsey who, as the story goes, was appalled to find that no accommodation had been arranged for him. Wolsey should have known he was out of favour but quite how badly he was only just to realise. Campeggio left in October to return with Henry's love letters to Anne that had been stolen from Hever, still in the Vatican archives to this day. He was never to return to England.

Wolsey had received a letter from Anne:

My lord,
Though you are a man of great understanding, you cannot avoid being censured by every body for having drawn on yourself the hatred of a king who had raised you to the highest degree to which the greatest ambition of a man seeking his fortune can aspire. I

cannot comprehend, and the king still less, how your reverent lordship, after having allured us by so many fine promises about divorce, can have repented of your purpose, and how you could have done what you have, in order to hinder the consummation of it. What, then, is your mode of proceeding? You quarreled with the queen to favor me at the time when I was less advanced in the king's good graces; and after having therein given me the strongest marks of your affection, your lordship abandons my interests to embrace those of the queen. I acknowledge that I have put much confidence in your professions and promises, in which I find myself deceived. But, for the future, I shall rely on nothing by the protection of Heaven and the love of my dear king, which alone will be able to set right again those plans which you have broken and spoiled, and to place me in that happy station which God wills, the king so much wishes, and which will be entirely to the advantage of the kingdom. The wrong you have done me has caused me much sorrow; but I feel infinitely more in seeing myself betrayed by a man who pretended to enter into my interests only to discover the secrets of my heart. I acknowledge that, believing you sincere, I have been too precipitate in my confidence; it is this which has induced, and still induces me, to keep more moderation in avenging myself, not being able to forget that I have been Your servant [32]

The writing was well and truly on the wall. On 8 October Wolsey was stripped of office and charged with praemunire – an offence against the king's supremacy by obeying papal authority – and on 27 October he was found guilty of high treason.

Bryan had been in France as Henry's resident ambassador while the aftermath of the failure of the legatine court played out. Henry had been concerned that Francis would not back his great matter or might even side with Charles V in protecting his aunt, Katherine. But Francis I assured Bryan of his continuing support. Charles V was no longer a threat when the treaty of Cambrai – the Ladies Peace – was signed on 5 August between

France and the Holy Roman Empire. More disconcerting was the Turkish invasion of Hungary. Other heads of state had more concerns than Henry's wish for a divorce.

Bryan was still with Francis in Paris, perhaps at the Louvre or the more favoured Saint-Germain outside the city, in October although Henry had given him leave to return to be replaced by George Boleyn and John Stokesley. Although they would not arrive till December with the instructions 'On their arrival at the French court they shall confer with Sir Francis Brian on the repair of Albany into Scotland, to interrupt the alliance between Scotland and the Emperor; on which subject, though Brian has been continually solicitous, the King has received from him no direct answer. They shall tell Francis that Brian is recalled to look after his own causes, and they are sent in his place'.[33] Finally Bryan could return home.

Katherine of Aragon

Chapter Five

Diplomatic Duties

1530–1533

The treaty of Cambrai allowed for the release of Francis I's sons, the Dauphin Francis and Henri, duc d'Orléans, held captive by Charles V in Spain for four and a half years, but in order for Francis to get them back he had to pay the Holy Roman Emperor 2 million gold écus. He had raised three quarters of the money but the rest he had to borrow from the king of England. This amount was actually owed to the English crown by the Hapsburg empire from Henry VII's time so Henry VIII allowed for this to make up the rest of Francis' payment thus cancelling the Hapsburg debt.

England had held the magnificent fleur-de-lys jewel in lieu of the payment owed. Maximilian, Holy Roman Emperor at the time and Charles V's grandfather, had pawned the Burgundian jewel for 50,000 crowns in 1508, which formed part of his wife Mary's dowry. 'The Fleur de Lys, the most respected symbol of the house of Burgundy, was decorated with countless diamonds, rubies, sapphires, emeralds and pearls, and held to contain pieces of the True Cross and even one of the Holy Nails'.[1] It was this jewel that Bryan was entrusted with returning to Charles V.

On 18 February 1530 Francis' ambassadors described it as 'so large and heavy that it is a horse-load so to speak. It is to be placed in a box, and sealed with the seals of the King of England, Bryan, the French and Imperial ambassadors, to be opened at the place and time to be agreed on, when the Princes are delivered. The king of England has commissioned the Grand Master, Mons. de Borges, the bishop of Bayonne, Turenne, and Bryan for the delivery of the jewel and indemnity, and to obtain a quittance of the Emperor'.[2]

Bryan was in France at Blaye, north of Bordeaux, by 8 March when it was reported to the Grand Master of France, Anne de Montmorency, that Bryan was awaiting his summons. Montmorency was in charge of the return of the French king's sons, and was currently staying in Bayonne. It took nearly a month before Bryan reached him. He had to stay with the jewel at all times and travel was slow with the roads in a poor condition. Henry wrote to Francis to thank him for treating Bryan so well and commented 'I don't know whether Bryan be more of an Englishman or a Frenchman.'[3]

The release of Francis' sons was delayed several times until finally on 1 July the boys were exchanged for the ransom at a halfway point on the river Bidassoa close to Fuenterrabia. As part of the treaty, Francis was to marry Eleanor of Austria, Charles' sister, and she accompanied the boys home. Henry was extremely concerned about what this marriage would mean for England and Bryan was advised to stay in France for the time being with his ear to the ground to find out more information.

In June the Duke of Norfolk wrote to Montmorency to thank him for the assistance he had given to Bryan but also to discuss the king's matter which had been debated at the university of Paris 'for whereas 56 doctors had been instructed on his side, and 7 on the opposite side, at the Congregation lately held there were 36 doctors opposed to his purpose, and only 22 on his side. This looks suspicious. I trust you will use your influence with your master to obtain the desired object at Paris'.[4] Henry was looking for more support for his divorce.

After Francis married Charles V's sister, Eleanor, at Roquefort-de-Marsan and the celebrations were over Bryan reported on the situation. He told the king that all was not well 'The French ladies mock the Spanish, and the Spanish ladies spy well. It is feared the Queen will not long agree with the French king's mother. Many favor the former out of spite to the latter.'[5] It was not to be a happy marriage and Henry VIII was content it posed no threat to his negotiations.

Bryan was recalled at the end of August and was back at court by 2 September. In his absence Henry had granted Bryan and the Marquis of Dorset the office of keeper of Sawsey (Salcey) forest, Northamptonshire and 'also power to make a coppice of 20 acres of underwood, and to sell the underwood yearly'.[6] But he was not back for long before Henry was informing Francis that Bryan would be returning to France in place of John Wellysbourn, gentleman of the Chamber. Bryan was in Calais by 27 October where he wrote to Sir John Daunce to be good to his friend Rocwoode, under-marshal of Calais 'sore charged with wife and children, who has done the King good service'.[7]

Thomas Seymour, brother to Jane Seymour, was employed by Bryan to carry his dispatches during his time in France. One such report sent from Blois was in reply to what Bryan had heard about Wolsey and his 'sinister practices'.[8] The cardinal had been arrested on 3 November and stripped of his office and property including Hampton Court Palace. His downfall was imminent.

I received at Blois, on the 19th, your letters under signet, dated York Place, 11 Nov., stating the detestable practices and conspiracies set forth by Wolsey, at Rome and within your realm, against your dignity. After I had studied them well I visited the Grand Master, who inquired, what news from England? and I learned from him that news had been received from the ambassador in England, — that the Cardinal was in hold, but for what offence he knew not; that the King (Francis), however, thought he deserved imprisonment. I told him that I had been sent to prevent any untrue surmises, with a letter from you to Francis and my Lady, desiring them that in event of hearing of this matter otherwise than was good, they should know the truth, "showing him that if the particularities, which I said did chiefly concern presumptuous sinister practices made to court of Rome for reducing him to his former estate and dignity, contrary to his faith, truth, duty and allegiance, were so well known to the King your brother, my lady and him, as they were to your Highness, there were no doubt but he and they would much abhor the same." He replied, they judged you to be so just a prince that you would not have punished the Cardinal but for his heinous deserts. He then took me to dinner with him, where dined the cardinal of Lorraine, the marquis of Saluce, the count St. Pôl, the count de Taunte, and the Imperial ambassador, "who showed to me there very good countenance, howsoever he thought."[9]

But it was not just about Wolsey. Bryan also reported the latest on the issue of the divorce:

Cannot discover that there is any towardness for a meeting between Francis and the Emperor. Asked the Great Master, who said fools did babble they wist not what....Francis has also told him, of his own accord, how the Venetian ambassador lately advised him to write to Henry, urging him to desist from his great matter as a thing that might not lawfully be done. To which he had replied that he spake unlearned, the matter having been examined by a great number of clerks in France and Italy, most of whom were on the King's side. The ambassador observed in answer, "that ever the most number were fools." "Then," said Francis, "your commonwealth of Venice, which is ordered by the most number, by your saying is governed by many fools." At this, according to Francis, he was much abashed, "showing me he was so aged he was waxen a child again, doating for age." Neither Pope, Emperor, nor Signory, should prevent him, he said, from acting in the King's behalf.[10]

Henry was convinced for the time being that he still had the French king's support.

Wolsey had left court for York but once there was accused of treason by Henry Percy, 6th Duke of Northumberland, once Anne Boleyn's suitor, and ordered to London. En route he became unwell at Leicester Abbey and died on 29 November 1530. Sir

Thomas More would take over as the king's Lord Chancellor. Bryan delivered the news to the French court but rumours were rife over Wolsey's demise. The Venetian ambassador Giustinian reported that the cardinal had tried to escape to Scotland and failing that had taken 'a phial containing a certain electuary he swallowed it and died'.[11]

On a lighter note, Bryan wrote to the king's ambassador William Benet in Rome on 20 December 'I pray you recommend me heartily to Signora Angela, and desire her to send me a pair of sweet perfumed gloves'.[12] Perhaps this was the lady who he had shared favours with during his time there.

The year 1531 was busy for Bryan in France and a nightmare for Henry who heard from the pope that he was forbidden to remarry until Clement VII ruled otherwise. He needed to be sure of Francis and it was Bryan's job to make sure the French king was committed to his cause.

In January Bryan was looking for an audience with Francis and wrote to Henry from Paris to assure him:

Went to court at St. Germain's on Monday, where the King was hunting. Returned there on Tuesday before the King was up. When he was up, and had heard mass, he mounted his horse for Paris, and dined at St. Cloud... Explained our commission to the King, who spoke of it with such affection as left nothing to be desired, and said we should ask nothing that would not be granted, and that to further your cause he would lose an ounce of blood to write with it to the Pope in his own hand.... the King said he would write so sharply to the Pope that he should know that Francis is your dear friend and good brother...The King, at his going away, said, "Let the Pope and Emperor do what they list, I will be the King my brother's friend, in spite of them all."[13]

This was welcome news to Henry but regardless on 11 February 1531 Henry VIII became Supreme Head of the Church in England

and Wales 'as far as the law of Christ allows'.[14] Henry could not rely on the pope and he was determined to have his divorce finalised and as quickly as possible.

Bryan met with Francis I again in March. 'I stirred him as much as I could, saying it was no surprise that he should be vexed at the Pope's treatment of his faithful friend and brother, but also make him an instrument to deceive you. On which he, seeming in a rage, said: "It shall not lie in the power of any, especially of none such as he is, to do so mischievous an act and engender suspicion between us"'.[15]

And he also passed on gossip adding:

Here follows a passage in cipher about the French king's treatment of his Queen, and his open preference for Hely (Anne de Pisseleu). On the day when the Queen entered Paris, he rode to a house where Hely was, and set her before him in an open window, talking two hours with her in sight of all the people.[16]

He wasn't exactly talking to her but behaving much more intimately and on his queen's coronation day no less. Francis I's behaviour with Anne d'Heilly, later Duchess of Étampes, was causing a scandal and Bryan told the king 'being both in one house they lie not together once in four nights; another he speaks very seldom unto her openly; another, he is never out of my lady's chamber... he has also divers times ridden six or seven miles from the Queen and lain out four or five days together, as it is said, at the houses of his old lovers'.[17]

Bryan was with Francis I again in April and had heard that the Pope might become more favourable to Henry's cause. Charles V's ambassadors had arrived and received a cold reception which would be pleasing for Henry to hear, but Bryan had also heard rumours that the Holy Roman Emperor may have been planning to invade England. Henry wrote to Bryan in July that he had sent a letter to Clement VII 'for speedy determination of his cause'[18] and sent Bryan a copy. But by September when Bryan was at Compiegne he was reporting that 'little favor is expected from the Pope'.[19]

Thomas Cranmer, later Archbishop of Canterbury, had come to the attention of the king with his idea that Henry should look to university theologians across Europe for their opinion on his divorce. Several diplomats were sent off to do just that headed by Edward Foxe, Provost of King's College and previously Wolsey's secretary. Foxe was with Bryan in France when Bryan informed Benet in Rome, that they had the 'determination of the canonists of Paris' and that the book of Orleans was in the hands of the king of England. Benet was also looking for expert opinions and reporting back to Foxe who would gather all the evidence into two volumes *Collectanea satis copiosa* (The Sufficiently Abundant Collections) and *The Determinations.*

Henry was losing patience with the pope and told his ambassadors Ghinucci, Benet and Casali in October that it might be time to leave Rome. 'We do not think that our ambassadors should attend the court of one who shows such hostility to us'.[20]

In November 1531 Bryan was hunting with Francis in Hainault after which Henry informed him he was sending Edward Foxe to him 'as matters of importance have arisen requiring the knowledge of the Latin tongue, which is wanting in Sir Francis'. A note was added to keep secret between themselves – Bryan, Foxe and Tayler.

They are to be very diligent in learning news of that Court, without creating suspicion. The King has heard from Flanders that the meeting between the Emperor and the French king is still talked of. Some say there are preparations at Cambray, and the Emperor is going to Tournay for that purpose. He trusts so much in the honor of the king of France that he believes there is no truth in this rumor, but would be glad to have it contradicted by the King himself. They are to keep watch upon this, and not to think it tedious, as they will be relieved in a few days... The Almoner is then to return to England, and Brian as soon as the French king leaves the parts adjoining the Emperor's dominions, and no meeting takes effect.[21]

Francis made no attempt to meet with Charles V or his ambassadors and so Bryan and Foxe were back in England by 21 December and Benet had returned from Rome. Chapuys reported 'many suspect that the Pope will not do all that the King asks him'.[22]

Bryan was back at court to receive New Year's gifts of a cup and bowl, goblets and salts and was back in the privy chamber by April 1532 when Henry issued new instructions for who was to attend him. There were two groups of seven to each serve six weeks in every twelve. Bryan was included with 'My lord of Rochefort, Masters Hennage, Nevell, Russaile, Welsborne, and Henry Knevet'. 'My Lord Marques [Dorset], Masters Norrice, Carewe, Browne, Cheyney, Page, and Weston made up the other group'.[23]

Bryan would have a quieter year in 1532 with no diplomatic journeys abroad. There was a time for more pleasure and relaxing with the king playing bowls, cards and dice which he often won. Anne Boleyn was frequently at their games and enjoyed beating the king at the 'Pope Julius' card game. Bryan's brother-in-law Henry Guildford had made an enemy of Anne by openly speaking against her and opposing the king's desire to annul his marriage to Katherine. Anne had sworn she would see him lose his position as comptroller of the king's household when she became queen to which Guildford replied she need not bother and he would resign himself. Henry, however, would twice refuse his resignation and tell him to ignore women's talk. But time was running short for Guildford and although he kept up his duties despite Anne's dislike of him, he died in May.

In October Bryan was with the king at Stone in Kent from where he wrote to Thomas Cromwell, newly elected to the Privy

Council and a rising star at court after the loss of Wolsey:

The King has given the French queen's skinner a protection for one year, which he sends with this. Desires Cromwell, if his debt pass not 40 marks, to aid him to the said grant; otherwise the King's pleasure is that he shall retain it till he speak with him.[24]

Although it was only a small matter it is the first recorded letter between Bryan and Cromwell – a correspondence that was to last throughout Cromwell's life. Bryan was an astute courtier and knew who to keep on side and when to step away from those about to fall but his own position was now in question.

He was not asked to accompany the king and Anne, newly created Marquis of Pembroke, to France when they set off to sail from Dover. Although it seems he was to be in the retinue travelling to Calais, he was replaced by Carew. Chapuys reported 'the Grand Esquire (Carew) will go tomorrow, instead of Brian, to wake up the French, and tell them that the King has started'[25] but we have no clue as to why Bryan was replaced.

The meeting didn't go exactly to plan anyway with Francis I's senior ladies including his queen Eleanor, Katherine of Aragon's niece and sister Marguerite d'Angoulême refusing to meet Henry's paramour. The king spent four days with Francis at Boulogne whilst Anne stayed in Calais but the French king returned with Henry for a great banquet on 27 October where Anne made her splendid entrance as the chronicler Hall recorded:

After supper came in the Marchiones of Penbroke, with. vii. ladies in Maskyng apparel, of straunge fashion, made of clothe of gold, compassed with Crimosyn Tinsell Satin, owned with Clothe of Siluer, liyng lose[loose] and knit with laces of Gold: these ladies were brought into the chamber, with foure damoselles appareled in Crimosin satlyn[satin], with Tabardes of fine Cipres[cypress lawn]: the lady Marques tooke the Frenche Kyng, and the Countes

of Darby, toke the Kyng of Nauerr, and euery Lady toke a lorde, and
in daunsyng[dancing] the kyng of Englande, toke awaie the ladies
visers, so that there the ladies beauties were shewed.[26]

But Hall also had more to say and wrote that on their return to
England the couple married on Thursday 14 November 1532
'The kyng, after his returne maried priuily[privily] the lady Anne
Bulleyn on sainet Erkenwaldes daie, whiche mariage was kept so
secrete, that very fewe knewe it, til she was greate with child, at
Easter after.'[27] This may have just have been a betrothal as they
were also married in the King's private chapel at Whitehall Palace
on 25 January 1533. Anne was pregnant and Henry was still
technically married to Katherine.

Henry had to wrap up his great matter quickly and Thomas
Cranmer, archbishop of Canterbury and previous resident
ambassador to Charles V, was instructed to hold an ecclesiastical
court at Dunstable Priory in May along with the bishops of
Winchester, London, Bath and Lincoln. Bryan was one of those
chosen to deliver a citation to the queen, living now at Ampthill,
asking her to attend. He would later testify to her reaction to her
summons. Chapuys reported:

...the Queen has been cited to appear before the archbishop of
Canterbury on the first of next month, at an abbey 30 miles from
here. This being a solitary place has been chosen for secrecy, as
they fear that if the affair were managed here, the people would not
refrain from speaking of it, and perhaps from rioting. The citation
at first threw the Queen into great perplexity, not knowing what to
do; but after I had given her my advice she did not care for it. There
is no danger for the Queen in anything they can do, if she does
not renounce her appeal, expressly or tacitly, and by some indirect
means, which the King and his ministers are attempting by various
methods. To remedy this I have drawn up certain protestations,
whereby I hope that the Queen will not fall into the net of their

calumnies and malice.[28]

Katherine refused to attend the court that opened on 10 May but it allowed Cranmer to declare her contumacious – wilfully in contempt of court. Bryan's testimony was central to his declaration.

This Monday, on depositions made and taken before me by Mr. Briane, Gage, and Vaux, my fellows, your Grace's servants, and upon the words spoken by her at the serving of the monition, I have pronounced her vere et manifeste contumacem; so that she is, as the counsel informed me, precluded from more monition to appear. I shall therefore make further acceleration in my process than I thought I should. I desire credence for Mr. Brian, to whom I have declared my further mind.[29]

On 13 May 1533, Thomas Cranmer, Archbishop of Canterbury, declared Henry and Katherine's marriage null and void and on 28 May he declared Henry and Anne's marriage valid.

Bryan missed his cousin's coronation on the 31 May as he had left for France with Thomas Howard, the Duke of Norfolk. Their aim was to stop Francis from meeting with the pope fearing what the outcome could be for England. Henry told Norfolk however that 'Sir Fras. Brian and Sir John Wallop (were) to repair with him to the interview, provided they never present themselves to the Pope'.[30]

Bryan's friend Lord Lisle, Arthur Plantagenet, was about to assume the role of Lord Deputy of Calais and was shipping over his goods in order to take up residence. Both Bryan and the duke enjoyed his hospitality provided by his servants and 'continually sent at every meal for beer and wine, both French wine and Gascon, whereupon I caused your yeoman of the cellar, Petley, to give attendance upon them at their commandment, both early and late, and so he doth right well'.[31] Bryan sent his thanks before they journeyed on. This is the first extant letter in the Lisle Letters between the two of a correspondence that would last for seven years.

Bryan was also building up a relationship with Cromwell whose accounts list an award payable to him of £200 in June at the same time Bryan was informing him of their progress in France from Moulins.

I perceive that the French king intends to meet the Duke at Ryon in Auvarne (Auvergne), instead of at Notre Dame de Piesse, and will send a gentleman to conduct him through the country, who is expected at Moleyns tonight or tomorrow night, and the Duke will leave when he arrives. Today the French king left Lyons (in his pilgrimage to Notre Dame de Piesse), and is going with all speed to Ryon, which is only 15 leagues from Moleyns. Afterwards he will go to Notre Dame de Payse. Norfolk has been hitherto marvellously well treated, and I think his treatment will be no worse, but every day better. Recommend me to my friends in the Court, and to the King when you have leisure with him, if you think it convenient.[32]

In July the pope threatened that Henry would be excommunicated unless he put aside Anne Boleyn and reinstated Katherine as his queen. Bryan took the news to Francis I at Rodez near Toulouse and asked for his support. Francis intervened and the pope agreed to give Henry until September to restore his queen which of course the king would never do.

Bryan moved on to Marseille where he heard the news that Queen Anne had given birth to the Princess Elizabeth in September. His mother Lady Margaret would shortly take over the running of her household. Whilst there he wrote to Lord Lisle:

Although we have despatched the courier in great diligence, yet we have detained him that we might write this. We abide here with evil wines the Pope's coming, as the hawk prieth for her prey. He is not expected yet for seven days. His stuff is come, and two of his cardinals are within eight leagues: hence great preparation is made for him. The legate of France, the Great Master, and a great number of the French nobles and gentlemen are here awaiting his arrival; the French king himself being at La Baine, four leagues hence. When we shall depart we cannot tell, but we hope to leave about the end of this month, "against which time I, Sir Fras. Bryan, desire you to make more ready for me a soft bed than an hard harlot." We would you had part of the wines we drink here, and then you would pity us. Commend us to my Lady, Master Porter, and other friends.[33]

Bryan was ever mindful of the king's business but he was certainly fond of his wine and women! We don't know what Lisle replied but by the end of October Bryan was writing again joking about their misliving:

Sir, whereas in your last letter I perceive that in Calais ye have sufficient of courtesans to furnish and accomplish my desires, I do thank you of your good provision. But this shall be to advertise you that since my coming hither I have called to my remembrance the misliving that ye and such other hath brought me to; for the which being repented, have had absolution of the Pope. And because ye be my friend, I would advertise you in likewise to be sorry of that ye have done, and ask my Lady your wife forgiveness, and, that forgiveness obtained, to come in all diligence hither to be absolved of the Pope.[34]

And again he turned to his wine:

Would God ye had as good wine Greek, wine amyable, and wine corse, as we have here. Of those two last my lord of Albany hath given me two barrels, which be much better for a preparative to cause a natural turn than the feeble strength of your three halfpenny beer that ye bib off there; but on this condition that we had some of your wholesome furs of England, or else England upon our backs to keep us from cold; for we be fain to walk in our unlined gowns.[35]

Bryan was present on 28 October when Francis I's son Henri married Catherine de Medici in the church of Saint-Ferréol les Augustins in Marseille. Bryan didn't think much of her looks 'which gentlewomen nor mistress be not as fair as was Lucresse' but there was certainly much celebration and another excuse to drink more wine which Bryan taunted Lisle was much better than his 'three halfpenny beer'. He was also feeling the wintry weather telling his friend he wished he had some wholesome furs from England 'upon our backs to keep us from cold, for we be fain to walk in our unlined gowns'.[36]

Francis met with the pope in October and November and inevitably Henry's divorce was a topic of conversation. Francis asked for a further suspension of the papal bull that would excommunicate the English king but Clement VII would only agree to another month rather than the six months Francis suggested.

In November, still in Marseille, Bryan was telling Lisle, 'No news here but that dead men be more plenty than quick capons'.[37] There was nothing more for the ambassadors to do but return home. Bryan stopped off to see his friend at Calais where he asked Lady Lisle for her dog Purquoy (from the French *pourquoi* meaning why) as a gift for his cousin and queen.

Returning home he met with the king and filled him in on his recent travels also passing on Lord Lisle's request for the revictualling of Calais. Anne was delighted with the present of the little dog 'which was so proper and so well liked by the Queen that it remained not above an hour in my hands but that her Grace took it from me'.[38] Bryan had seen through the tumultuous times that saw Henry's divorce his first queen and marry his second but there were far more challenging times to come.

Anne Boleyn

Chapter Six

The Fall of a Queen

1534–1536

Lord Lisle in Calais had sent his man John Husee to England on business and in January he was reporting that he had delivered the king's New Year gift, £20 in gold, with Bryan present. At some point Bryan asked Husee to remind Lisle that he promised him a barrel of herring and a hogshead of wine. Husee dutifully wrote to Lisle and told him 'Since my coming I have found more friendship to my lord in Mr. Brian and Mr. Kingston than in any others'.[1] Lord Lisle and his wife Honor Grenville, Lady Lisle, kept up a frequent correspondence with Bryan and looked for his patronage.

But in February there was an undisclosed matter that Bryan couldn't help with:

> ...he thinks the matter to lie so highly upon my lord's honour that he is loth to move the King in it. He broke the matter to Mr. Kingston, who would not advise him to do so. He promised to write to your ladyship, but he has had so much business that as yet I could not come by it. I see he has no mind to speak of it.[2]

These were quiet months for Bryan when he spent much time with the king. In March the papal court declared Henry's marriage to Katherine was still valid and the king was not in a good mood. Bryan took off to spend some time in Buckinghamshire but was back to have dinner with Nicholas Carew and Francis Weston at Thomas Goodrich's house, in April, on the same day the Nun of Kent, Elizabeth Barton, was executed at Tyburn.

Goodrich was made Bishop of Ely on 19 April by Cranmer. He was supportive of the reformation and had added his opinion to those collected that Henry's marriage to Katherine was invalid. His new position meant the University of Cambridge was in his jurisdiction and was key to supporting Henry's divorce. The pope may have declared in favour of Katherine but Henry had his allies. This was a difficult time in which to have beliefs that opposed the king's. The Nun of Kent had prophesied Henry's death if he married Anne Boleyn and lost her life because of it. If Bryan had any sympathy he kept it hidden. He was Henry's man and would follow where he led.

Henry had a notion to visit Calais in August and in May Bryan gave Lord Lisle warning but asked he kept the information secret. 'And for the said time of the King's coming, I would not upon this my writing ye should take this for a precise knowledge, whereby ye might take hindrance in your provisions, for ye know the mind of princes sometimes change...'[3] and it did.

He also asked Lisle for another consignment of wine but it seems there was a problem to the point none could be found that was 'meet for him'. One Anthony Cave had tried to procure the wine but:

> As my lord had given orders that no wine should pass out of Calais into England, some wine bought by Mr. Cave for him could not be forwarded. My lord is displeased, and wonders who so informed Mr. Bryan, as no one came to his lordship to ask for any licence to have wine out for him. Mr. Cave denies to me that he ever wrote to master Bryan of any such matter, and has written to Bryan himself requesting him to vindicate him to my lord.[4]

Hopefully Bryan stuck up for Anthony and found his wine elsewhere!

Lisle did not have an easy time with the administration of Calais. He had to make sure the town was defended and provisioned, see that the soldiers garrisoned there were paid, be available to entertain visiting nobles and keep order amongst the English officials.

Part of his job was to give rooms to the Calais 'spears', young men of standing and wealth, for which there was a lot of competition made more complex by the king giving out rooms as gifts. Lisle had to manage the list of prospective spears and when a room became vacant, the next man on the list received a place but it was not as easy as that with the king giving grants and the rooms being bought and sold amongst the spears.

Lisle had a difficult relationship with Sir Richard Whethill, the mayor of Calais. In 1531 Henry had granted his son Robert the next vacancy and by 1533 his father was complaining that he still hadn't been given it. It came to a head in 1534 when Whethill followed Lisle into his garden and raged at him. Their wives too also fell out with Lady Whethill verbally attacking Lady Lisle whilst at church.

He had asked Cromwell for advice but was just told to put them in prison, something in reality he could not do. This was the mayor and his wife, well respected in Calais and the argument caused a divide between those who lived and worked in the garrison town.

Lady Whethill took it upon herself to go to court and complain to the king about Lisle. Bryan had received correspondence from his friend and hearing he was being slandered wrote off to him quickly from Woodstock where he was with the king.

I perceive that there is a certain variance betwixt young Whethill and your lordship concerning the Spear's room that John Cheyney had, which as I understand you have given unto one Wynebank who, as your lordship saith, hath done the king good service. The said Whethill pretendeth to have abill signed for a Spear's room of the next avoidance. Amd whereas your lordship saith that the said Whethill saith that he hath a bill signed only for Highfield's room or any privy seal, whereby it appeareth that he hath it for Highfield's room or any other. I have moved the King's Highness to know his pleasure herein... and his Grace willed me to write unto you that his pleasure is ye shall suffer the said Wynebank to continue in the said room until such time as you shall know further of his grace's pleasure on your behalf.[5]

Robert Whethill had been at court too and was also slandering Lisle. Bryan cautioned his friend:

The said Whethill saith the contents of your letters be not true, and he will prove the same by sufficient record and witness. Wherefore mine advice and counsel is, ye send hother as shortly as you can some honest man further to open and declare unto the King's Highness your demeanour towards the said Whethill, with a bill signed with the hands of them which heard the words betwixt your lordship and him.[6]

Lisle's man Husee also kept him up-to-date with news from court and warned him that the Whethill's had friends in high places but that Bryan and Norris 'your lordship's unfeigned friends' were doing their best to help him. They had also counselled that he obey the King's letters as Lisle would do but the complaints against him rumbled on. Bryan told his friend to 'be merry' but he also offered the advice that Lisle should 'shew yourself to be the King's officer and be not afraid of no man in doing right and justice' telling Lisle that 'amity bindeth' him to write so plainly he also advised him to look to his household as 'you are no good husband in keeping of your house, which is a great undoing of many men'.[7] The affair would result in a commission hearing the following year where Lisle would be accused of selling rooms and taking bribes but although he may not have dealt with the situation well, there was no taint of corruption. Although there were later attempts for Robert Whethill to obtain his room, he never did.

The Lord Chamberlain and Captain of Guînes, William Sandys, had also complained about Lord Lisle failing to carry out his duties in Calais and Husee later reported:

> *Mr. Bryan says that you must keep all things secreter than you have used, for nothing is said or done there that is not known at Court; and you must assume more of the King's deputy and not use the company of mean persons, which is not for your honor.*[8]

The situation would only worsen for Lisle but Bryan tried over the coming months to support his friend at court.

There were certainly changes afoot. Henry had had an affair this year with an unnamed 'Imperial lady'[9] which had led to arguments between himself and Anne Boleyn. Some have posited that this may have been Jane Seymour, another cousin, whom Bryan had been responsible for placing in the queen's household but it was not otherwise reported that Jane had gained the king's affections as yet. Bryan however may have seen the writing on the wall for Anne. He noticed how unpopular she was and how the king was taking his pleasures elsewhere which may have led to his argument with Anne's brother, George, Lord Rochford, in December over which he had the king's support. Chapuys reported 'that the King has lately shown favour to Master Bryan in a suit he had with the said Rochford'.[10] Could Bryan have been distancing himself from the Boleyns already?

For the moment Bryan had other issues to occupy his time. George Throckmorton, a politician and MP, wrote to him in January 1535 that he had heard the king was displeased and urged Bryan to intercede for him and gain him audience with the king. Throckmorton was a staunch supporter of Katherine of Aragon and against Henry's divorce. He was often in trouble and Cromwell had told him to 'stay at home and meddle little with politics'.[11] There were many who asked for Bryan's help as he was so close to the king. He couldn't save them all and if he helped this time he was unable to save Throckmorton from the trouble he found himself in in the next couple of years when his loyalty was questioned for supporting the Northern Rebels and for having links to Reginald Pole.

As justice of the peace for Buckinghamshire Bryan heard the case of George Taylor of Langwich in February. The man was accused of slandering the king saying 'The King is but a knave and liveth in avowtry, and is an heretic and liveth not after the laws of God,' and further, 'I set not by the King's crown, and, if I had it here, I would play at football with it'.[12] Taylor denied he had said those words but if he had it would be due to drunkenness. Bryan wrote to Cromwell recommending Taylor be 'hanged, drawn and quartered, and his quarters set up in Buckingham, Aylesbury, Wycombe and Stony Stretford. Thinks the due execution of justice in this case will be a very great example and the safeguard of many'.[13] We don't know if Taylor was executed. His sentence may seem harsh but the Bishop of Lincoln would praise Bryan for 'the good order he has taken in Buckinghamshire in redressing the heresies hitherto used in this woody country of Chiltern'.[14]

Bryan's hard work did not go unnoticed and in March he was granted 'the foundation, site, and precinct of the late monastery of St. Mary the Virgin, Ravenston, alias Raunston, Bucks; a water-mill in the town of Ravenston, 20 messuages, 40 acres of land, 40 acres of pasture, 200 acres of meadow, 100 acres of wood, 10l. rent in Ravenston, Weston, Pedyngton, and Stoke Goldyngton, Bucks'[15] all previously belonging to Cardinal Wolsey. He also asked Cromwell just days afterwards for the preferment of the prior of Chicksand Priory in Bedfordshire. Despite all his acquisitions he still had his debts including £100 he owed to the duke of Suffolk.

Back in November 1534 Bryan had sworn an oath under the Act of Supremacy that recognized Henry VIII as the Supreme Head of the Church of England. An oath of loyalty was required not only to show outward acceptance of the king's new role but to confirm allegiance to Anne Boleyn. Although Bryan's support for the queen had been wavering he took the oath as many others did but those who refused – including John Fisher and Sir Thomas More, executed in June and July – paid the price. It was a stark reminder not to get on Henry's bad side.

Others looked to Bryan to help them. Cromwell had begun his assessment of the monasteries and churches prior to their dissolution. Robert Neckham, prior of Worcester Abbey, was disliked by his fellow monks who accused him of mismanagement. He asked Bryan to intercede on his behalf with Cromwell who had been contacted by the disgruntled monks. Whatever Bryan did worked and Neckham kept his position.

But Bryan was now to leave local politics to one side as Henry sent him to France in November 1535 with Stephen Gardiner and Sir John Wallop. Henry was concerned with France's growing relationship with Paul III, who had assumed the role of pope after Clement VII's death in 1534.

He arrived in Calais on 23 November and informed Cromwell he had been 'as syke a see man as ever passed see'[16] but was to soon hear the news that the rule of the Duchy of Milan, after the death of Francis Sforza, was contested by Francis and the pope which would lead to hostilities between them and lessen the risk of any threat to England. Bryan told Cromwell in December that he thought he had little to do in France as events were panning out.

And events were changing in England too. Katherine of Aragon died in January 1536 at Kimbolton Castle removing any fear of war with Charles V. Living in the fenlands of Cambridgeshire, the queen had been ill for some months with few servants to care for her and kept apart from her daughter. The damp, marshy environment had hastened her end.

Chapuys, the Spanish ambassador, had managed to visit the queen but feeling she was on the mend, had returned to London. Now in mourning for the woman he had so long fought to help he told the Holy Roman Emperor:

The Queen died two hours after midday, and eight hours afterwards she was opened by command of those who had charge of it on the part of the King, and no one was allowed to be present, not even her confessor or physician, but only the candle-maker of the house and one servant and a "compagnon," who opened her, and although it was not their business, and they were no surgeons, yet they have often done such a duty, at least the principal, who on coming out told the bishop of Llandaff, her confessor, but in great secrecy as a thing which would cost his life, that he had found the body and all the internal organs as sound as possible except the heart, which was quite black and hideous, and even after he had washed it three times it did not change color. He divided it through the middle and found the interior of the same color, which also would not change on being washed, and also some black round thing which clung closely to the outside of the heart. On my man asking the physician if she had died of poison he replied that the thing was too evident by what had been said to the Bishop her confessor, and if that had not been disclosed the thing was sufficiently clear from the report and circumstances of the illness.[17]

Chapuys suspected poison had been used to bring Katherine's life to its final conclusion and given that the king was relieved rather than upset over her death, he had his suspicions that the Boleyn faction had something to do with it. Nothing was proved and it is more likely that she died of cancer. In a final insult, she was buried at Peterborough Abbey as a Dowager Princess, not as Queen of England. Disgusted by this slight, Chapuys refused to attend.

Just days after on 24 January, Henry had a jousting accident that left his councillors fearing for his life. Chapuys reported 'On the eve of the Conversion of St. Paul, the King being mounted on a great horse to run at the lists, both fell so heavily that everyone thought it a miracle he was not killed'.[18] Henry was unconscious for two hours afterwards. This may well have resulted in a head injury that would affect the king's personality and behaviour over the coming years. He would certainly never joust again and the once active king would begin to rapidly gain weight.

However Henry soon recovered and it was not long before rumours abounded of Henry's infatuation with Jane Seymour, the daughter of Sir John Seymour and Margery Wentworth. Chapuys described her as being 'of middle stature and no great beauty, so fair that one would call her rather pale than otherwise'.[19]

The Life of Jane Dormer, Duchess of Feria, an autobiography, recalls that Bryan had tried to arrange a marriage in 1534 between Jane Seymour and William Dormer, but Jane had remained unmarried and as another of Bryan's cousins he continued to look out for her well-being. As the king became more enamoured of this plain and quiet young lady, the complete opposite of his wife, Anne Boleyn slipped into disfavour.

Anne had a fiery temper and could see what was going on. Her failure to provide Henry with his longed-for heir and her recent miscarriage had put her in a precarious position.

The Concubine had an abortion which seemed to be a male child which she had not borne 3½ months, at which the King has shown great distress. The said concubine wished to lay the blame on the duke of Norfolk, whom she hates, saying he frightened her by bringing the news of the fall the King had six days before. But it is well known that is not the cause, for it was told her in a way that she should not be alarmed or attach much importance to it. Some think it was owing to her own incapacity to bear children, others to a fear that the King would treat her like the late Queen, especially considering the treatment shown to a lady of the Court, named Mistress Semel [Seymour], to whom, as many say, he has lately made great presents.[20]

It was said Anne had found Jane cosying up to the king and screamed at Henry 'I saw this harlot Jane sitting on your lap while my belly was doing its duty!'[21] Her jealousy drove her into a rage but she could not have imagined how serious her fall would be.

In April 1536 Bryan told Jane's family 'they should soon see his niece well-bestowed in marriage'.[22] Some believe he was part of a faction along with the Carew's, Seymour's and Courtenay's that sought Anne Boleyn's disgrace. If he was actively working to bring her down he would have been walking a fine line. Henry may have been interested by Jane but up until accusations were brought against his queen he probably only wanted her as his mistress rather than his next wife.

Much has been written about Anne's downfall and feelings are mixed as to how much she was set up or whether there was any truth in the accusations against her. So much evidence is missing that we shall never really know but what did happen were five men were charged with adultery with the queen; Mark Smeaton, Henry Norris, Sir Francis Weston, William Brereton and George, Lord Rochford, her brother. Only Smeaton confessed and probably only because he was tortured.

Bryan's friend and fellow ambassador Thomas Wyatt and Richard Page both spent some time in the Tower accused but never charged. And Bryan was 'sent for in all haste on his allegiance'.

A later deposition by the abbot of Woburn told the story:

At the fall of queen Anne Mr. Bryan was sent for by the lord Privy Seal in all haste "upon his allegiance." At his next repair to Ampthill the abbot went to visit him, being in the Court with lord Grey of Wilton and others. Sir Francis espied the abbot at the gate, and of his gentleness came to meet him. Said, "Now welcome home and never so welcome." He, astonished, asked, Why so? Said he would explain at leisure. Afterwards, in the great chamber with the others, drew a parallel between the fall of Lucifer and that of queen Anne, congratulating Sir Francis that he was not implicated. He replied it was true that when he was suddenly sent for he marvelled;

but knowing his truth to his prince he never hesitated but went
straight to my lord Privy Seal, and then to the King, and there was
"nothing found" in him.[23]

Bryan had been questioned but found innocent of any misdemeanour. It had been a close call.

On 5 May Carew and Bryan 'in his newly turned coat'[24] arrived to give Sir William Kingston, constable of the Tower, a message from Lady Rochford to enquire after her husband, George Boleyn, Lord Rochford. In it she told him she would 'humbly make suit unto the king's highness for him'.[25] It may have been a comfort in his last hours but Jane herself has testified against him and the king would not be averted from Anne's downfall running its course and taking five men with it.

Mark Smeaton, Sir Henry Norris, Sir Francis Weston, Sir William Brereton and Lord Rochford were executed on 17 May. Bryan was included as a debtor in the list Weston made as he prepared for death. Bryan had spent many an evening playing cards or dice with both Weston and Norris and must have felt their passing, but he was the king's man and to keep his favour life had to go on. He was given Norris' position of chief gentleman of the privy chamber and benefitted from forfeited revenues. In a letter Cromwell wrote to Stephen Gardiner assuring him of £200 out of the £300 of the pensions paid to Norris and Lord Rochford he commented 'the third hundred is bestowed of the Vicar of Hell'.[26] Gardiner was not best pleased he had to share this income with Bryan.

This is the first time Bryan is referred to as the Vicar of Hell, a nickname that would stick. The Catholic recusant Nicholas Sander would later write that it was because of his 'notorious impiety' that the king also referred to him thus. Sander wrote, 'This man was once asked by the king to tell him what sort of a sin it was to ruin the mother and then the child. Bryan replied that it was a sin like that of eating a hen first and its chicken afterwards. The king burst forth into loud laughter, and said to Bryan, "Well, you certainly are my vicar of hell"'.[27]

Anne was executed on 19 May and it was Bryan who was 'sent in all haste'[28] to tell Jane Seymour the news. Chapuys caustically reported 'So Briant told Mrs. Semel and other ladies on the day the King sent to inform her of the putain's condemnation; and though Brian is French in his leanings, he does not forbear to praise your Majesty in these matters, and to abuse and laugh at the French, who had made a foolish and shameful reply about the combat between your Majesty and the king of France'.[29]

Jane Seymour married Henry on 30 May at Whitehall and was proclaimed queen on 4 June. She was known to have been sympathetic to the late Queen Katherine and her daughter Mary. Mary's followers saw Jane as a way to return the princess to her father's favour. Mary had refused to acknowledge her father's marriage to Anne Boleyn and they saw a chance to return his daughter to her former glory. Bryan's sister, Lady Carew, warned her 'in all things to follow the King's pleasure, otherwise she was utterly undone'.[30] The act of succession in March 1534 had excluded Mary and placed Anne Boleyn's daughter before her but now Elizabeth was in the same situation as Mary as another act of succession passed in July 1536 put the rights of any children born to Jane Seymour first.

Bryan appears to have been in discussions with Mary's supporters including Sir Nicholas Carew, Sir Anthony Browne, Sir Thomas Cheyney and Lord Morley, Lady Rochford's father. The Marquess of Exeter and Sir William Fitzwilliam were seen as the ringleaders of Mary's faction and dismissed from the Privy Council in June whilst Anthony Browne and Bryan were questioned in June of their knowledge of 'any conventicle devised by any one for the advancement of the lady Mary'.[31]

Bryan admitted that he had discussed the Lady Mary in general with his fellows of the Privy Chamber 'saying that they rejoiced that the King had escaped this great peril and danger, and that the issue the King might have, if he took another wife, should be out of all doubt; but if the King wished to make an heir-apparent in defect of such issue, they thought lady Mary was meet if it stood with the King's pleasure'.[32]

He also mentioned a conversation he had had with Elizabeth Darrell, Thomas Wyatt's mistress, who wanted his help in receiving 300 marks Queen Katherine had bequeathed her and to seek a place in Jane's household 'seeing she saw no hope in the lady Mary, for she heard say that she would not be obedient to the King'.[33]

Bryan reported the gossip and nothing more. And contrary to Darrell's feeling that Mary would not obey her father she signed a document on 15 June acknowledging Henry as Supreme Head of the Church and admitting his marriage to her mother had been 'incestuous and unlawful'.[34]

It seems like there was still some suspicion or rumours concerning Bryan. In July, Cromwell wrote to Stephen Gardiner that he perceived Gardiner was 'somewhat pained at what Cromwell wrote about Brian. Thinks the matter had better drop now, seeing that it has come to a good end, both for the King's satisfaction and for the removal of any bitterness between them'[35] or he could have been referring back to Bryan's interrogation.

Bryan was hunting with the king in August and all was well between them. The king saying 'naughty bruits were soon blown'.[36] Henry was in a good mood after killing twenty red deer. But the king's mood would soon sour when he heard news of a rebellion.

By October, dissent in the North culminated in an uprising in Lincolnshire. The religious changes that Henry had enacted to allow his marriage to Anne; his break with Rome and the establishment of the new Church of England plus the dissolution of the monasteries, all added to the rebel's grievances. Up to 50,000 Catholic men from Louth and the surrounding Lincolnshire towns of Caistor, Grimbsy, Yarborough, Market

Rasen and Horncastle marched on Lincoln and occupied Lincoln Cathedral. They demanded the right to worship as Catholics and that Lincolnshire churches would be protected from desecration.

Henry had sent the duke of Suffolk north but at Huntingdon he 'found there neither ordnance nor artillery nor men enough to do anything; such men as are gathered there have neither harness nor weapons. Begs that ordnance, and artillery, and a thousand or two of harness may be sent with speed'.[37] Hoping that he would be supplied soon, he nevertheless sent a message to the rebels to warn them of 'the greate slaughter that ys like by stroke of sworde whiche ys p(re)payrede shortly to ensue among(es) you'.[38] Suffolk continued on to Stamford by which time he had around 3000 men at his command. On 6 October a letter was dispatched to Bryan from the king instructing him to assemble his men at Kimbolton and to join up with Charles Brandon and his men. Suffolk needed his help and wrote to the king 'Sir Francis Bryan with his band and his company, shall come and resort hither unto me at all speed'.[39]

Henry VIII sent the rebels a message concluding 'We charge you, eftsoon, upon the foresaid bonds and pains, that ye withdraw yourselves to your own houses, every man; and no more to assemble, contrary to the laws and your allegiances; and to cause the provokers of you to this mischief to be delivered to our lieutenant's hands or ours and you yourselves to submit to such condign punishment as we and our nobles shall think you worthy.'[40] They were faced with the wrath of the royal army (although much smaller than their own) and charges of treason if they did not disperse.

Bryan occupied Stamford and began the interrogation and pardoning of the rebels with Sir William Fitzwilliam, back in favour after being questioned about the Lady Mary. Fitzwilliam was eager to retain the king's favour and was 'so earnest in the matter that I dare well say that he would eat them with salt'.[41] They reached a quieter Lincoln on 18 October. Fearing the wrath of the king's army, the rebels had already dispersed. Several of the insurgents were captured including the vicar of Louth and Captain Cobbler, two of the main ringleaders who now awaited execution. Bryan was dispatched back south with reports for the king at Windsor.

The Lincolnshire rising had fizzled out but now there was trouble in Yorkshire. Robert Aske, a London barrister, originally from Richmond, North Yorkshire, led his growing band of men to York. The rebellion was known as the Pilgrimage of Grace and was the largest and most severe Henry had ever faced during his reign. Aske, with his followers, wanted the dissolution of the monasteries to stop and England to return to Rome. Theirs were religious grievances but there were also political and economic factors; poor harvests, unwelcome taxes, the loss of Katherine as queen, and the rise of the much disliked Thomas Cromwell, the king's secretary and chancellor. It was not the king they blamed as such but men like Cromwell whose evil policies had changed the country. The rebels sought change and were well organised. Their banner was of Christ's five wounds and they all took an oath to their cause.

Ye shall not enter into this our Pilgrimage of Grace
for the commonwealth, but only for the love that ye do bear
unto Almighty God his faith, and to Holy Church militant
and the maintenance thereof;
to the preservation of the King's person and his issue,
to the purifying of the nobility,
and to expulse all villein blood and evil councillors
against the commonwealth
from his Grace and his Privy Council of the same.
And that ye shall not enter into our said Pilgrimage
for no particular profit to yourself,
nor to do any displeasure to any private person,
but by counsel of the commonwealth,

nor slay nor murder for no envy,
but in your hearts put away all fear and dread,
and take afore you the Cross of Christ,
and in your hearts His faith,
the restitution of the Church,
the suppression of these heretics and their opinions,
by all the holy contents of this book.[42]

Bryan headed back north to hear Robert Aske and his rebels had taken York and laid siege to Pontefract Castle. He returned to Lincoln to gather his men to lift the siege but by the time he got there it had fallen. Its guardian Lord Darcy had informed Henry of their precarious position as the rebel troops amassed around them 'The insurrection has so increased all over the North that we are in great danger of our lives and see no way how it can be repressed'.[43] Darcy surrendered along with the castle inhabitants and took the Pilgrim's oath. Henry was not impressed.

The Duke of Norfolk and the Earl of Shrewsbury were sent by the king to meet with over 30,000 agitators near Doncaster. The king's army was vastly outnumbered and to avoid the potential for mass slaughter, Norfolk promised the crowd that all would be pardoned if they dispersed. Aske agreed, if the king would address their demands, including that a parliament should be held at York or Nottingham, that the Princess Mary should be declared legitimate, suppressed monasteries be restored to their former state, Papal authority re-established and Cromwell removed from power.

Whilst a truce was issued for the king to consider the rebel's proposals Bryan was sent on to Newark to check its defences. He reported to Suffolk in November:

Within four miles there are two fords within two butts' lengths of each other, at which 40 horse at one and 25 at the other might cross abreast. If no rain come in these days it will not be up to the knee. There are also two above the town as ill. If the water increase not it will be impossible to defend them. The water has fallen since Sunday nearly a fathom and a half. If the rebels come, we should lose ourselves and the King's artillery if we trusted to the fords. Have six passages to keep and the bridge, which we could hold against all their power if the fords were sure...The castle here has scant lodging for 100 men, and there is no water. Advises him to inform the King of this. No men would venture their lives to serve their master with better will than they, but with the water in this state it is not possible.[44]

Whilst at Newark, Bryan had sent one of his men to York to spy on the rebels and he reported to the king:

I, Sir Francis Bryan, sent a servant, kinsman of my old friend John Knyght's, to spy; at York he was near taken, but, saying he was Sir Peter Vaffesser's (Vavasour's) servant, escaped; at last he was brought to Aske and recognized, so he said he sought for a priest of mine "that had robbed." Aske's answer appears in his letter to me, herein enclosed. "I know him not nor he me, but I am true and he a false wretch, yet we two have but two eyes; a mischief put out his t'other."[45]

Aske, leader of the rebels, fell for the story that Bryan's servant was looking for a thief and wrote to him offering his help. But the matter didn't end there. Sir Peter Vavasour asked Bryan's servant to appeal to Francis Bryan to petition the king to pardon Aske. Bryan passed on the information that Aske would be looking for a pardon but he in no way supported the rebel.

The Duke of Suffolk sent Bryan back to Henry in November after he had examined the Trent fords with Sir John Russell. 'If I could have undertaken this journey he should not have gone, nor would he unless that I charged him upon his allegiance'[46] and he was with the king at Richmond at the beginning of December.

He had to return to the Duke of Norfolk with instructions to prolong the truce but was soon back with his king.

On 6 December the Duke of Norfolk was presented with the pilgrim's '24 articles' at Doncaster. In it they asked for a general pardon, religious reform, that parliament would be held in York or Nottingham, that the Lady Mary be made legitimate and that 'Lord Cromwell, the Lord Chancellor, and Sir Ric. Riche to have condign punishment, as subverters of the good laws of the realm and maintainers and inventors of heretics'.[47] Norfolk agreed to the parliament at York and a pardon for those involved in the rebellion. The other matters would be passed to the king. Aske, being happy that Henry had listened to their demands and change would occur, disbanded the rebel army. Of course Henry had his own ideas but for now the threat of rebellion was over and Aske was invited to spend Christmas with the court at Greenwich.

During the Christmas celebrations Henry had a task for Bryan. Although Lady Mary had been allowed back at court since October the king asked Bryan to help him test his daughter's virtue. He had heard that Mary knew 'no foul or unclean speech'[48] and couldn't believe she was so innocent. He persuaded Bryan to dance with her at a masque and mention a sexual swear word. As Bryan whispered scandalous words in her ear, Mary paid no attention and Bryan could subsequently tell the king his daughter was truly virtuous. Or perhaps as many a time before he told the king exactly what he wanted to hear.

Princess Mary

Chapter Seven

A Time of Ill favour

1537-1538

Bryan was sent to France on 8 April 1537 to ask Francis I for the arrest and extradition of Cardinal Reginald Pole, the author of *Pro ecclesiasticae unitatis defensione* (*Defence of the Unity of the Church*) which strongly denied Henry's supremacy and urged him to return to the Catholic Church and the pope's authority. Henry had supported Pole – the son of Sir Richard Pole, who had been chamberlain to Prince Arthur – in his career in the church and paid for his education but he left England in 1532. Reginald had initially supported Henry in his divorce but when the king asked him to confirm the legitimacy of marrying his dead brother's wife and his thoughts on papal authority, Pole's response was his *Defence of the Unity of the Church* in which he lambasted Henry in the strongest terms. 'You have squandered a huge treasure; you have made a laughing stock of the nobility; you have never loved the people; you have pestered and robbed the clergy in every possible way; and lately you have destroyed the best men in your kingdom, not like a human being, but a wild beast'.[1] Not what Henry was waiting to hear and the king wanted him back in England to answer for his traitorous words.

Pole had been informed by Francis I when he reached Paris that he was unwelcome and the cardinal had soon left for neutral Cambrai. Henry was furious that Bryan had missed him in Paris and had been unable to persuade Francis to incarcerate him. He wrote to tell Bryan 'Your presence might have quickened our good brother against Pole, and you could then have reported if Pole had any secret access to the (French) king's presence'.[2]

On 21 April, the bishop of Faenza, papal nuncio in France,

was reporting:

Brian, the new English ambassador, who being a favourite of that King never comes here for anything [not?] very important, came to make a last effort to get the Legate into his hands and bring him into England, into the catalogue of the other martyrs. Not having succeeded, he is very desperate, and as discontent as possible with the French, and brags, saying that if he found him (the Legate) in the midst of France he would kill him with his own hand, and similar big words. This shows clearly the mind of that King, and how necessary it is that the Legate should take care of his life, having to deal with fools and wretches, and that they fear [him] more, as I gather from him (the Legate), than anything else from Rome.[3]

Henry was growing desperate and exasperated with Bryan for not fulfilling his duty. He wrote to his ambassadors 'And for as much as we would be very glad to have the said Pole by some mean trussed up and conveyed to Calais, we desire and pray you to consult and devise between you there-upon. If they think it feasible, Brian shall secretly appoint fellows for the purpose'.[4] A letter from Sir Thomas Palmer, Knight Porter of Calais, to Cromwell suggested that Bryan had chosen him to apprehend (possibly kill) the cardinal and Palmer had been sent the sum of £100 for the purpose.

But when nothing had been accomplished by 18 May Cromwell wrote to Gardiner and Bryan:

Touching your further proceeding for the apprehension of his traitor Pole... his Highness perceiving by the rest of your letters that his intent therein is so disclosed, or at least suspected, that being the said Pole thereupon advertised, as ye write he is, to take heed of the preservation of himself, there is no likelihood there ye should be able to conduce that matter to his desire, his Majesty mindeth not to advance any money for his said apprehension.[5]

However there was still a possibility that if Bryan or Gardiner could convince someone else to capture Pole that they should 'promise them some honourable reward'[6] and the king would provide the funds. Presumably Sir Palmer had returned to his position at Calais. Bryan had certainly met with him there previously on a flying visit to arrange Pole's capture and borrowed his horse to return to the French court.

It was becoming too well known that Bryan might use nefarious means to do away with the cardinal in his desperation to please the king and the cardinal had been warned and was still hiding in Cambrai where he 'doth not come out of his lodging'.[7] Henry could see Bryan would not be able to fulfil his mission and he was recalled in June.

Bryan must have taken the opportunity to see Lisle on his way through France. Husee reported from London in April that the king had been troubled by his leg and seldom went out. He assured Lisle that 'It were good your Lordship did speak earnestly unto Mr Bryan at his return, and make him your friend in all such things as your Lordship shall have ado here at the Court; for surely, if he set in his foot with his good mind, he hath no fellow now in the Privy Chamber'.[8] Bryan would be a good friend and 'stick to'[9] Lisle. But there would be only so much that Bryan was willing to do.

Whilst Bryan had been in France, Robert Aske, the leader of the Northern Rebellion, had been examined and found guilty of high treason. Another rising, Bigod's Rebellion, had broken out in Cumberland and Westmorland when it became obvious Henry would not make good on any of the pilgrims demands. Sir Francis Bigod, who had served Wolsey, led the rebellion which Robert Aske did not condone and tried to stop. But the king had had enough and it gave him the excuse to punish all those that had risen against him.

The Duke of Norfolk was ordered to end the rebellion in the north for once and for all. 'You must cause such dreadful execution upon a good number of the inhabitants, hanging them on trees, quartering them, and setting their heads and quarters in every town, as shall be a fearful warning'.[10] Over 200 rebels were executed, including Aske, throughout the summer and the risings finally ended. John Hussey, previously chief butler of England, was one of those men executed and Bryan took on his role being paid an extra £600 a year. It was a huge increase in his income and he oversaw all aspects of supplying the king's table from ordering to storage to collecting the duty on imported wines – probably his dream job since he was in charge of wine, wine and more wine!

Bryan also returned to his role as justice of the peace for Buckinghamshire and reported to Cromwell in July on the case of 'a fray between one of the shoemakers of Stony Stratford and the organ-player of the town'.[11] They were indicted for rioting and remained in gaol awaiting the king's pleasure but Bryan thought it would be the end of the matter as 'the country (is) in such good stay that no further inquiry need be made'.[12]

He also let Cromwell know of the condition of the county given the sweating sickness was running rampant.

I cannot see what way the King can come to Grafton. I hear they die at Reading, and am sure they do at Thame and also within a mile of Mr. Williams' house at Buckingham. The King might come from Esthampstead to Bishops Owburne, thence to Berkhampstead, 12 miles, thence to Eston, ray lady Bray's, 7 miles, for neither my Lord nor my Lady is at home. Then to Whaddon, 7 miles, and thence to Grafton, 7 miles. These houses would be sufficient for the King as the Queen is not coming, "and, thanked be God, all clerear as yt" (clear air as yet). They die at Tosseter very sore. Orders should be given that none of the King's servants nor of the town "come there." Stony Stratford, Northampton, Brickhill, Hanslap, Olney, Newport Panell, Woburn, Dunstable, St. Albans, Ampthill, Hitchin, and Hertford, are as yet clear, Tyddington somewhat infected. If the King please, he may go from Ampthill to Hitchin, and so to Hertford, and on to Hunsdon.[13]

In October he was at Ampthill with the king. Lady Lisle had asked for his help in placing her daughter Katherine in the queen's or Lady Mary's household. Husee reported 'I have no hope of help from my lord Privy Seal or Mr. Bryan, as it is only a lady's suit. As to her preferment to my lady Mary, plain answer is made that her Grace shall have no more than her number'.[14] Mary was back in favour but Henry would keep strict control of her and her household.

Whilst at Ampthill, Bryan did try to help out one Sir John St John 'a man of gentle nature'[15] whom Henry had given the property of Bushmead Manor. He wrote to Cromwell that Bushmead 'lay so near his house that if he should be driven to remove he could find no place so meet. I am sure his name was entered in the book, but I hear Mr. Gasgyne labours for the same in recompense of the land he exchanged with the king'.[16] Mr Gascoigne had already approached Cromwell about the property and he took his side in the dispute. Although Bryan had tried to help he had been unsuccessful this time. To be close to the king didn't always mean that favours were granted.

On 12 October Queen Jane gave birth to Henry's longed-for son, Edward. Finally he had his heir. There was much rejoicing and Bryan attended the new prince's christening on the 15th at Westminster. In gratitude Jane sent him a gift of gold chains. But Henry's third wife was not to live to see her son grow up. Within days she died at Hampton Court palace possibly of puerperal fever.

Bryan was ill himself in December and had to stay in Canterbury until he recovered but by January 1538 he was well enough to be sent on another embassy to France. Henry was concerned with Francis' relationship with the emperor and with the breaking of their treaty. Bryan was also to discuss a further marriage for Henry. The king had his eye set on Marie de Guise who had been promised to his nephew James V but Francis could not be swayed from his course and Bryan was recalled.

In March Bryan was back at Ampthill with the king and around this time Lord Lisle sent his stepson George Basset to serve his friend. The boy was settling in well and 'every man praiseth him for his towardness and good conditions'.[17] He would be a great asset to Bryan and accompany him on his diplomatic missions.

He was sent back to France in April with Thomas Thirlby, bishop of Westminster, to continue building the relationship between Francis and Henry and also to look at the possibilities of who could be Henry's next wife. He stopped at Calais en route to see his friend Lord Lisle and continued on to Paris but soon he was receiving instructions to travel on to Nice where Francis and Charles V were to sign a truce brokered by the pope. Once there he met up with Thomas Wyatt, now ambassador to Charles. Francis was refusing to talk to the English ambassadors and Bryan spent his idle time drinking and gambling to the point Wyatt had to lend him £200 for his debts, captured in his poem 'How to use the Court and Himself Therein' – a spending hand that always powreth owte, had need to have a bringer in as fast.

Bryan was enjoying himself though and wrote to Lord Lisle:

These Courts been so full as all the world were gathered upon a plump. The Emperor's Court is great, the bishop of Rome's less, and the French Court three times so big as the most of them." All the towns and villages within four or five leagues of them are so full that one can hardly get a lodging. "And in the French Court I never saw so many women; I would I had so many sheep to find my house whilst I live. And great triumphs in all these Courts have been made, and many meetings of all parts but of the Emperor and the French king, for they yet meet not; nevertheless yet have they concluded a truce for ten years and thus been departed, the Emperor determining towards Spain, the French king homeward, and the bishop of Rome towards Rome.[18]

Wyatt would later write of Bryan:

> *To thee, therefore, that trots still up and down*
> *And never rests, but running day and night*
> *From realm to realm, from city, street, and town,*
> *Why dost thou wear thy body to the bones?*[19]

Bryan was a well-known ambassador, used to wearing out his bones in service to his king but the French had become wary of him after the Pole debacle and his time as French ambassador was coming to a close. Castillon wrote to Francis:

> *You must to Bryant make more than usual demonstration of your amity for the King your brother, without, however, letting him know you have heard so much, for there is nothing, even to a look, he does not write to the King his master. You know in how many ways suspicious men judge of others. Bryan had an audience with the king in July who bragged of his new friendship with the emperor. Bryan asked him 'Sire, is my master no longer your friend?' To which he replied 'Yes, certainly (as I am) also the friend of the emperor'.*[20]

Francis' reply in July mentioned however that Bryan had left Nice 'very well satisfied with Francis'. And here he touched on the other matter that Bryan had broached that of Henry meeting with a selection of possible brides in Calais. Francis 'would be glad to have the King marry in France; but to send him as Brian suggested Mesdemoiselles de Vendôme, de Lorraine and de Guise with Francis' sister, would be unreasonable. Better let him send some good and honest personage to see the King's cousins'.[21] And that would not be Bryan who swore 'Hitherto I have been a good Frenchman, but now I am going away determined to stand by my master'.[22] Francis had lost his faith in the English ambassador and

Bryan had felt his coldness. He would soon be called home.

Henry was not happy either. The French ambassador found the king 'more ill pleased than I have found him for a long time'.[23] Bryan's diplomatic mission had no positive result. Bryan informed the king 'On coming home, will have to declare to him honey with gall. The matter is too long to write'.[24] He was probably unaware that Henry was furious with him and had heard the reports of his behaviour in France. He would never return to the French court.

Bryan was back in England at the end of August but was 'sore sick of a burning ague'[25] and his doctor asked Cromwell to send 'Master Michell the physician'[26] to cure him. He became so ill it was thought he would not recover. Castillon reported 'As to the return of Maistre Bryant, he got such a bad reception from his master that he is quite ill in bed, as the King himself told me, who said he was a drunkard, whom he will never trust'.[27]

He was out of favour and the king had ordered Cromwell to look into Bryan's accounts but he did send his physician. Gradually he regained his strength and Henry's anger abated although Bryan lost his position as chief gentleman of the privy chamber and the position was given to Anthony Denny who had previously been in his own household.

And there had also been some trouble while he was away.

Robert Hobbes, a friend of Bryan's, and abbot of Woburn abbey in Bedfordshire, had acknowledged the king as supreme head of the church, but had later changed his mind and insisted 'the part of the bishop of Rome was the true way'.[28] In May 1538 he had been taken to the Tower with his fellow monks and investigated.

Bryan had had many conversations with him and knew his allegiance had changed. In Hobbes testimony he spoke of Bryan mentioning one time when they discussed religion:

Last Lent at Ampthill, after Sir Francis had entertained him and others of the country, he saw a Bible of the New Translation in Sir Francis' bed chamber, and said it was not well interpreted in many places, which might lead to much error. Sir Francis said that interpreters must sometime follow the letter and sometime the sense, and pointed out the words in Luke of the consecration of the blessed body and blood of Christ. The abbot said that was well set out.[29]

But nothing he said implicated Bryan as sharing his beliefs about the king's supremacy and Cromwell did not take the matter any further. The abbot however was executed and Bryan lost a friend albeit one that had spoken against the king.

Also while he was away in July the Earl of Westmoreland had written to Cromwell. 'Yesternight was brought to me on suspicion one James Prestwych, who said he was Sir Francis Bryan's servant, "with broken writings"'. Bryan had employed Prestwych as schoolmaster to the royal wards. He was carrying a letter written in Greek and wearing Bryan's livery but when told he would be questioned by Cromwell felt that 'if he came to you afore his master came home he should lose his head'. The earl could get nothing out of him and the prisoners final words were 'I see it is God's will that I should be taken here, and if I die I shall die for my faith.'[30] What the writings were and the man's fate are not known but it may have added to suspicion over Bryan's dealings.

After his behaviour in France and the things that happened in his absence he was walking a fine line with the king which must have added to his sickness but he soon began to rally and regain his energy.

In 1 September Bryan was writing to Cromwell, having much to thank him for:

Dr. Myhell arrived here last night and showed me your Lordship's letter to him, authorising him by the King's command to come to me in my extreme sickness. I had before Dr. Cromer, who has taken great pains with me, but I must abide the will of God. Your great kindness and the coming of the Doctor have revived me, and I desire to live to do you some service in recompense. I would write more but for extreme pain and lack of good remembrance. This gentleman, who has taken great pains with me, both beyond the seas and here, will report more fully.[31]

Lord Lisle was anxious to hear how his friend faired and sent Husee to visit him. He was pleased to report he was much amended and was 'never more healthful nor merrier' telling Lisle's man of a dream that he had had that Henry had made him Comptroller of Calais 'only to keep your Lordship happy'.[32]

Bryan had weathered the storm and by the end of the year was back at court. His wishful motto *ja tens grace* – I hope for salvation – said it all.

Reginald Pole

Chapter Eight

A Tale of Two Queens

1539–1542

Although Anthony Denny had replaced Bryan as chief gentleman of the privy chamber, Bryan was still listed as one of Henry's men in January 1539. The previous year might have dented his reputation but he was still close to the king and had rooms assigned to him when he was at court. When not serving the king, Bryan was living at Woburn. After its abbot was executed, the abbey was dissolved being divided between John Williams who received the manor of Utcote and Francis Bryan who received Whitnoe Grange, south of the abbey, the abbey site, the coney warren and great pond. John Husee reported to Lisle that Bryan was not at court in April but was back by May when he gave the king a gift of peascods from Honor Grenville, Lady Lisle.

The court was a dangerous place to be as Henry's irrationality and bad humour grew as he got older. The Exeter Conspiracy was a suspected plot by the Pole and Courtenay families to overthrow the king and place Henry Courtenay, 1st Marquess of Exeter on the throne. Castillon, the French ambassador, had reported, 'The king told me a long time ago he wants to exterminate the House of Montague that belongs to the White Rose, the Pole family, of which the cardinal is a member. So far I don't know what he means to do about the Marquess [of Exeter, Henry Courtenay]. It looks as if he is searching for any excuse he can find to destroy them.'[1]

Not only did Henry's paranoia play a part here but Cromwell too was eager to see the powerful Courtenay fall. The 1st Marquess of Exeter, the king's cousin, was a wealthy landowner in Devon and Cornwall and had been a gentleman of the privy chamber and one of Henry's closest companions. He had also joined the Privy Council and was constantly at odds with the reformist Cromwell. His wife, Gertrude Blount, had served Katherine of Aragon and was a committed Catholic. She had hated the treatment of her former mistress and was warned in 1533 along with her husband to 'not trip or vary for fear of losing their heads'.[2] It was well known where Courtenay's religious tendencies lay although he was loyal to his king. He had been one of the supporters of the Lady Mary that had been questioned along with Bryan and Carew over their support. And his beliefs gave Cromwell a lever to pry him from the king and bring down other conservatives at court.

Geoffrey Pole, Cardinal Pole's brother, had been arrested on 29 August and under interrogation he implicated the marquess and marchioness of Exeter and Henry Pole, 1st Baron Montagu, amongst others as wanting 'a change in this world without meaning any hurt to the king'.[3] What Geoffrey reported was all conversation and rumour. There was nothing concrete. No hint of an actual rebellion being planned or any action to unseat the king but given the Treason Act had made it an offence to even speak against the king what he had to say was enough to bring the marquess of Exeter, Lord Montagu, Sir Edward Neville and others to trial.

Montagu was purported to have said things like 'The king is not dead, but he will die one day suddenly. His leg will kill him and we will have jolly stirring' and 'I like well the doings of my brother the Cardinal'. Exeter that 'knaves rule about the king. I trust to give them a buffet one day'. Sir Edward Neville, Henry Pole's brother-in-law, was reported to have said 'his highness was a beast and worse than a beast'.[4]

They were all found guilty. Sir Edward Neville, was beheaded on 8 December 1538 followed by Henry Courtenay, 1st Marquess of Exeter. On 9 January 1539, Henry Pole, 1st Baron Montagu, followed them to the block. Reginald Pole was attainted in absentia. His mother Margaret Pole, Lady Salisbury, would also be imprisoned and later charged. Geoffrey Pole was pardoned and released although he attempted suicide twice. The marchioness of Exeter was imprisoned and released in 1539 but her son Edward would remain in the Tower until Mary's accession in 1553. Henry, Montague's son, who had also been imprisoned, was last seen in the Tower in 1542.

Bryan's friend and brother-in-law, Nicholas Carew, was also investigated and charged with treason for nothing more than his association with Henry Courtenay on 14 February 1539. Bryan appalled at the thought, was called to sit at his trial.

Sir Nic. Carewe of Bedyngton alias of Westminster, knowing the said Marquis to be a traitor, did, 20 Aug, 1537, at Westhorseley, Surr., and at other times, falsely abet the said Marquis, and, 24 Aug 1537, and at other times, had conversations with him about the change of the world, and also with his own hand wrote him divers letters, at Bedyngton, 4 Sept 1537 and at other times, and the said Marquis at that or other times sent divers traitorous letters to the said Carewe from Westhorseley which the said Carewe traitorously received, which letters they afterwards, to conceal their treason, traitorously burnt at Westhorseley and Bedyngton, 1 Sept, 1539 and at other times; and afterwards, knowing that the said Marquis was indicted as aforesaid, 29 Nov, 1539 the said Carewe at Bedyngton traitorously said these words in English, "I marvel greatly that the indictment against the lord Marquis was so secretly handled and for what purpose, for the like was never seen".[5]

Carew was found guilty. It is not recorded how Bryan felt about his friend's death on Tower Hill but he must have grieved for his loss and thanked his lucky stars that he had managed to escape Henry's ire over the years. The charges against Carew had been spurious and it was rumoured that the real cause of his death was that he had offended the king and Cromwell. Chapuys believed it was really because he was one of Lady Mary's supporters. Whatever the truth Henry put to death one of Bryan's, and his own, closest companions.

Bryan's sister Elizabeth, Carew's wife, had to give up Beddington Hall, their family home, where Jane Seymour was housed before her marriage to Henry. She now had to rely on her brother to help and house her and Carew's son and four daughters. She would write to Cromwell also to help her retain some of their property. Henry had after all given it to both of them on their marriage.

In the most humblest wise I beseech your lordship to be good lord to me and my poor children, to be a mediator unto the king's grace for me, for my living and my children's' and that your lordship would speak to his grace, that I may enjoy that which his gave me, which is Bletchingly and Wallington, trusting that his grace will not give it from me. And I humbly desire your good lordship to speak a good word to his grace for me, that I may enjoy it according to his grace's grant. And, to advertise your lordship, I have but twenty pounds more of my husband's lands, which is a small jointure; and if he had not offended the king's grace and his laws, I should have had an honest living, which should have been the third part of his lands; but now I cannot claim that, by reason that he is attained. I trust his grace will be good to me and my poor children, to reward me with some part of it. Also, I humbly pray your good lordship to speak to his grace to give me the lands in Sussex, which is in value six score pound and ten, to that I have by his grace and my husband, altogether amounteth a little above three hundred marks, the which I ensure your lordship I cannot live honestly under. All that I have had in my life hath been of his grace, and I trust that his grace will not see me lack; but whatsoever his grace or your lordship shall appoint me, I both must and will be content. I pray your lordship not to be miscontent with me for this my bold writing, to put your lordship to so great trouble and pains. And for your lordship's aid,

help and furtherance in this my suit, you bind me and my children
to pray for your lordship and to have our poor hearts and services
during our lives. And thus the Holy Ghost have you in his keeping,
and send you long prosperous life.[6]

Lady Bryan, their mother, sent thanks to Cromwell so he had
managed to help her. She would lose Beddington, given to Walter
Gorges, and Bletchingly but would retain Wallington and although
it was in 'great decay' she would make her home there.

My lord, I most humbly thank your good lordship for the great
goodness you showed my poor daughter Carew, which bindeth me
to owe you my true heart and faithful services while I live. She sends
me word that it is the king's pleasure she shall have lands in Sussex,
which is to the value of six score pounds, and somewhat above,
which I heartily thank his grace and your lordship for; but, good my
lord, there is never a house on it that she can lie in. Wherefore, an
it would please the king's grace, of his most gracious and charitable
goodness, to let her have that his grace hath appointed now, and
Blechingly, which his grace gave her without desiring of her part,
which grieveth her sore to forego it. And if it will please his grace
to let her have those two, to her and to her heirs males, she shall be
the most bound to his grace that ever was woman; for then I trust
she shall be able to live and pray for the prosperous life of his grace
and all his, and you, my good lord, and somewhat to comfort her
poor children withal, which hath no succour but of the king's grace
and you, my lord, most tenderly beseeching your good lordship of
your goodness now to comfort two troubled hearts; for, my lord,
unfeignedly you have, and shall have our true prayers and hearty
service during our lives. Alas! my lord, nothing have I to comfort
her withal, as your lordship knoweth what case I am in, but only
to sue to your lordship for her and hers, which I, being her mother,
and she being so kind a child to me as she hath been, I cannot for
pit do no less. My lord, next the king's grace, in your lordship is all

our trust, or else I durst not be so bold to troublel you with these matter; beseeching you, my good lord, take no displeasure with me that I so do.[7]

Bryan helped her as much as he could but was soon caught up with other matters and was frequently writing to Cromwell himself. In February it was to inform him Sir Robert Lee, a previous High Sheriff of Buckinghamshire, was dead and that he hoped he would show favour to his second wife, Lettice Peniston, who had been brought up with his mother, Lady Margaret. In March he was championing one William Barbar who had been arrested on suspicion of counterfeiting a penny of twopence, but Bryan had found nothing when he searched his house at Horwood and felt 'It would be a pity to send him to gaol as your Lordship commanded if he be innocent'.[8]

He was expected back at court in April at a time when England was on full invasion alert. Defences were being prepared against attack after the pope began to rally support for Henry's excommunication across Europe. New ships were built for the navy and extra fortifications added along the south coast. Panic ensued when fifty of the emperor's ships were spotted off the coast but they were just on their way to Spain. A general muster was called and on 8 May Henry reviewed the troops at Whitehall:

When it was known that the king would see the Muster, Lord how glad the people were to prepare, and what desire they had to do their Prince service, it would have made any faithfull subjects heart to have rejoiced. Then every man being of any substance provided himself a coat of white silk, and garnished their basinets (helmets) with turves like caps of silk, set with ouches (gems), furnished with chains of gold and feathers: other gilted their harness, their halberds and poleaxes. Some, and especial certain goldsmiths had their breast plates yea and their whole harness of silver bullion.[9]

But all the preparation came to nothing as neither Francis I or Charles V had any intention of invading England on the pope's behalf. Even though Reginald Pole, Henry's nemesis, was now doing his best to rally support against the king he felt had become a tyrant.

In May 1539 Henry produced his Act of Six Articles, a statement of religious belief that showed distinct Catholic leanings. Protestants termed it the 'bloody whip with six strings' and saw it as a blow to the reform they had all hoped for. It came at a time when Henry had been negotiating for the hand of Anne of Cleves and courting the German princes, who had formed the defensive Schmalkaldic League against the Holy Roman Emperor, in case he had need of allies. The princes were unhappy with the Articles as a statement of faith, hoping that Henry would align with their more Protestant sympathies, but the king would not back down and the ambassadors continued to negotiate his next marriage.

In July 1539 Alexander Alesius wrote to Cromwell that:

There has been for some days at Wittenberg an Englishman who calls himself a kinsman (conjunctus) of Sir Francis Brian. Philip (Melanchthon) says he was also at Frankfort, and was there seen by Christopher (Mont). Here there was a suspicion that he was a spy of Cardinal Pole, for he said he had been a long time in Italy, and some papers of his were found in which he had noted many things for the Pope against Luther. If he write anything thither, do not believe his fables.[10]

This may have brought Bryan under suspicion again but in July and September George Bassett was reporting to his stepfather Lord Lisle that Bryan and his wife were in good health. Bryan was in fact with the king at Ampthill in Bedfordshire in September. Ampthill was one of the king's favourite hunting grounds which gave him 'marvellous good health and clearness of air'[11] and Bryan had taken on the stewardship around 1525 when he also ordered that a lodge be built for him so when the king was staying at Ampthill Castle Bryan had his own accommodation. Henry had been unwell with ague but the Ampthill air was doing him good. He was recovering and had attended a masque 'and was as merry as he has been this good while'.[12]

In November a court case mentioned Bryan. Cranmer was investigating those associated with Adam Damplippe, a preacher who had turned up in Calais but had subsequently gone missing when his sermons were called into question.

One Geoffrey Loveday, a spearman of Calais, who was investigated had also served Bryan:

We are credibly informed that he was not at Calais during Damplippe's preaching, but attending on Sir Fras. Brian, then ambassador with the French king. Two other witnesses depose against him, but it does not appear that they can prove any heresy. The three suspicious witnesses testify the same thing against Turney, viz., that he was a maintainer of Damplip, and a setter forth of his erroneous doctrine.[13]

Loveday had indeed been in France in 'the train of Mr Bryan which is much increased since his coming hither'[14] and had been reporting back to Lord Lisle on the comings and goings of the French court. But the suspicion over him was enough from him to be dismissed from his position in Calais and sent to England to answer the charges against him. It seems like his service to Bryan was only during the time of his visit to the French king as he had reported to Lord Lisle and since Bryan had no connection to the preacher himself, he could not be charged. No more is heard of Loveday but Bryan was once more crossing to France in December – not as an ambassador but to meet Henry's new wife.

Back in October Cromwell wrote to Lord Lisle, governor of Calais, to improve the town especially the Exchequer House for

Anne of Cleves arrival.

The king's Majesty's pleasure is that you shall view his Grace's house here called the Exchequer, that with all diligence all things therein necessary to be amended may be undelayedly repaired... Furthermore, his Majesty would that you should cause the streets and lanes there to be viewed for the pavements, and where any default is, to give commandment to those which should repair the same to see it immediately amended, endeavouring yourselves to put all other things within the said town in the most honest and cleanly order you can devise...[15]

Lord Lisle had had his work cut out for him renovating the Lantern Gate, the main entrance to the town, tidying the tiltyard, repairing walls and cleaning the entire town before even the work of decoration, fresh paint and royal emblems could be undertaken.

Anne was the second daughter to be born to John III, Duke of Cleves and his wife Maria of Jülich-Berg and by marrying into Cleves Henry would have the protection of the German princes who had already formed an alliance against Charles V. After a long journey through the Low Countries, sometimes not travelling more than five miles a day, she finally arrived at Calais on 11 December.

She was greeted outside the town by Sir William Fitzwilliam, Earl of Southampton and Lord Admiral, dressed in robes of cloth of gold and purple, 'who had in his companie thirtie gentlemen of the king's household, as Sir Francis Brian, Sir Thomas Seimer (Seymour), and others, beside a great number of gentlemen of his owne retinue clad in blue veluet, and crimson satin, and his yeomen in damaske of the same colours. The mariners of his ship were apparelled in satin of Bridges, cotes & slops of the same colour. The lord admerall brought her into Calis by lantern Gate. There was such a peale of ordinance shot off at his entrie, as was maruellous to the hearers'.[16]

As they waited for calm sailing conditions Anne asked Fitzwilliam to show her a card game that Henry liked to play. 'And so my Lord William and I played with her at cent and Mr Morison, Mrs Gilmyn and Mr Wooton stood by and taught her to play. And I assure your Majesty she played as pleasantly and with as good a grace and countenance as ever in all my life I saw any noble woman'.[17]

Anne invited the nobles to her apartments for an evening meal but the lord admiral was concerned at the king's reaction to such informality as with the playing of cards but Anne assured him otherwise and the admiral with the Lords Howard, Hastings, Talbot, Grey and Bryan, Knyvet and Seymour spent a pleasant evening with the bride-to-be.

What Bryan thought of Anne he kept to himself. Perhaps he spoke to Lord Lisle, his old friend, who he was able to catch up with while they waited for the weather to change. He still had the governor of Calais' stepson George Bassett in his service and the fourteen-year-old boy was happy to be with him. Bryan had to escort Anne of Cleves to Deal and on to Rochester, accompanied by young George, but he left her entourage to ride to Greenwich to meet the king. He accompanied him back to Rochester for Henry's first infamous meeting with his bride.

Chapuys reported:

And on New Year's day, in the afternoon, the king's grace with five of his privy chamber, being disguised with mottled cloaks with hoods so that they should not be recognised, came secretly to Rochester, and so went up into the chamber where the said lady Anne was looking out of a window to see the bull-baiting which was going on in the courtyard, and suddenly he embraced and kissed her, and showed here (sic) a token which the King had sent her for (a) New Year's gift, and she being abashed and not knowing who it was thanked him, and so he spoke with her. But she regarded him little, but always looked out the window... and when the King saw that she took so little notice of his coming he went into another chamber and took off his cloak and came in again in a coat of purple velvet. And when the lords and knights saw his grace they did him reverence... and then her grace humbled herself lowly to the king's majesty, and his grace saluted her gain, and they talked together lovingly, and afterwards he took her by the hand and led her to another chamber where their graces amused themselves that night and on Friday until the afternoon.[18]

The king was not happy, declaring he loved her not, and despite ordering Cromwell to find a way out of the marriage, it went ahead in January 1540.

It is possible that Bryan was also experiencing marriage problems. There is a story that his wife Philippa had left the family home and was living at a convent at Canonsleigh Abbey in Devon. There is a Philippa Fortescue who was pensioned off in 1539 along with the other nuns but George Bassett reported twice in 1539 that Bryan and his wife were well. She may have returned home after the abbey's dissolution in February or this Philippa could have been a relative from her first marriage to John Fortescue.

George had told his stepfather, 'My master, Sir Francis Bryan which is (a) singular good master unto me, and my good Lady Bryan which is very good unto me also... are in good health'.[19] But the Lisles wanted him home. When Bryan did not send their son back they reiterated their need to have the boy returned. They were considering sending him to Paris to further his education but Bryan was loath to part with him. In February he told Lisle's man the boy would be with him in a day or two but over a week later George's sister was writing that George was in good health and still at court with Bryan.

Husee was prompted to write:

I perceive by Mr. Bryan is not very willing to part from Mr. George,

nor Mr. George would not gladly go from him; therefore Mr. Bryan
stayeth him here till he hear again your lordship's pleasure be
known... Howbeit, both your lordship and my lady, as Mr Bryan
shewed me, sent unto him word by divers that he should send Mr
George over unto you.[20]

It is the last we hear of George being mentioned in the Lisle Letters
and it is unrecorded when he returned to France. He would later
settle in Cornwall, on his late father Sir John Basset's estates, and
become a member of Parliament. Life for his stepfather however
would now take a turn for the worst.

In May Bryan's close friend Lord Lisle was imprisoned in the
Tower on suspicion of treason. Lisle's governorship of Calais
had not been easy. There had been financial difficulties with
Lisle constantly asking Bryan to approach the king on his behalf.
The fortifications always needed repairing and the garrison
needed paying. He had repeatedly fallen out with Cromwell
over religious reform and then there had been the Whethill affair
and the controversy over the selling of rooms.

A commission of enquiry was ordered into affairs at Calais.
Lisle was vindicated but during the investigation one Clement
Philpott, Lisle's servant was questioned, and he told them of a
plot to capture Calais for the pope through Reginald Pole (who
later denied he had anything to do with it). The main instigator
was Sir Gregory Botolf (Gregory Sweet Lips), Lisle's chaplain
from 1538, who had planned to take the Lantern Gate during the
time when herring was bought and sold and the guard on the
gate relaxed. Philpott was to take the gate from within Calais'
walls while Botolf attacked from outside. But Philpott had got
cold feet and after telling the commission of the plot was sent to
London. Botolf had slipped through their fingers in Calais and
was staying in Louvain out of the commissioner's reach.

Henry sent for Lisle on 17 April and he spent a month in
London attending parliament before his arrest on 19 May. The

king was not convinced of his loyalty or his part in any plot but he was not put on trial whereas Philpott and other conspirators were executed 4 August 1540 for denial of the king's supremacy. Lisle's wife, Honor and her daughters Philippa and Mary were also placed under house arrest in Calais. Lisle would spend the next two years in prison. Bryan worried for his friend but at the time there was nothing he could do.

He had at least good news when he heard he was nominated for the Order of the Garter in April and was invited to attend the St George's day feast but unfortunately he was not successful at this time or later when he was nominated again to join the Order.

Not long after Henry had his marriage to Anne of Cleves declared invalid, Bryan received gifts of clothes from the king along with one Culpeper whose story would famously be linked to Henry's next queen.

Henry married the young and lively Catherine Howard, on 28 July at Oatlands. Catherine was another cousin of Bryan's, through his grandmother Elizabeth Tilney's marriage to the 2nd Duke of Norfolk. Henry was forty-nine, Catherine, although her age is debated, probably in her late teens or early twenties. Her father was Edmund Howard, the third son of Thomas Howard, the 2nd Duke of Norfolk, which made her also Anne Boleyn's cousin. Catherine grew up in a household with ten other children, step-siblings and siblings, and was soon sent to live with her step-grandmother Agnes Howard (née Tilney), the Dowager Duchess of Norfolk. She was sent to court to serve Anne of Cleves in late 1539 where 'the King's Highness did cast a fantasy to Catherine Howard the first time that ever his Grace saw her'.[21]

On the same day as Henry wed Catherine, Cromwell was executed. His list of offences was long including treason, heresy and planning to marry Lady Mary but none were proved and he didn't even stand trial. He had angered Henry through his part in negotiating the Cleves marriage and annoyed him further when he could not help him wriggle out of it. Bryan had spent a lot of time with Cromwell and corresponded with him frequently. It was just further proof that it didn't matter how high you rose, the king could take you down.

And another of Bryan's friends was in trouble. Thomas Wyatt, fellow diplomat and poet, was arrested again in January 1541 on suspicion of disloyalty and treason. After Cromwell's death his papers had been searched and letters written by Bishop Bonner in 1538 were discovered in which Wyatt was accused of being in league with Reginald Pole. Wyatt was led to the Tower with his hands bound surrounded by twenty-four archers.

The French ambassador Marillac reported that two men were arrested and it would 'be difficult to learn the true cause of their taking, for, by a law made at last, they condemn people without hearing them; and when a man is prisoner in the tower none dare meddle with his affairs, unless to speak ill of him, for fear of being suspected of the same crime'.[22] Across Europe, the Henrician court was becoming known for its tyranny. Chapuys wrote 'No definite charge has been made against Wyatt and nothing proved against him but words, which would not have been noticed elsewhere; but these people are so suspicious they make mortal sins of trifles'.[23]

Wyatt spent his time writing and it was possible that it was now he wrote his poem to Bryan:

Sighs are my food, drink are my tears;
Clinking of fetters such music would crave.
Stink and close air away my life wears;
Innocency is all the hope I have.
Rain, wind, or weather I judge by my ears.
Malice assaulted that righteousness should save.
Sure I am, Brian, this wound shall heal again,
But yet, alas, the scar shall still remain.[24]

Dr Brigden has posited that the last two lines contain a coded message for Bryan to keep his secrets. It refers to a passage in the Book of Ecclesiasticus that reads 'As for woundes, they may be bounde up agayne, and an euell worde maye be reconciled: but who so bewrayeth the secretes of a frende, there is no more hope to be had unto him'.[25] They had certainly shared diplomatic duties and one can imagine many secrets.

It was not looking good for the poet. His household had been disbanded and his belongings taken by the Crown. But Wyatt was not going without a fight and using his unique command of words he penned his *Defence* which not only refuted what he thought would be the charges against him but appealed to his judges to remember the law.

But it was never read out at his trial – for there wasn't one – in March the new queen Catherine Howard intervened for his release and he was pardoned and back as ambassador by the end of the year. Part of the terms of his release included that he return to his wife, Elizabeth Brooke, whom he had been separated from for over fifteen years. Wyatt had made his home at Allington Castle with his mistress Elizabeth Darrell who bore him three children. It is not known if his mistress was still there when he returned home but it seems unlikely that Wyatt would return to his wife and in his will written in June 1541 it was Elizabeth Darrell that he made provision for.

Wyatt had had an amazing reprieve but others would not be as lucky. In January 1542 Bryan was at a meeting of the Privy Council to tell them what he knew 'touching the traitor that calls himself in France *the White Roose*'.[26] Reginald Pole was still causing Henry problems and the king was determined to extinguish his line. But he couldn't reach the man he most wanted and so he turned to his mother.

On 28 May Margaret Pole, Countess of Salisbury, was executed. The news not only shocked the people of England but reverberated around Europe. Margaret had spent over two years in the Tower, now aged and frail, the sixty-seven year old suffered a horrendous botched execution.

Found on the wall of her room in the Tower was:

For traitors on the block should die;
I am no traitor, no, not I!
My faithfulness stands fast and so,
Towards the block I shall not go!
Nor make one step, as you shall see;
Christ in Thy Mercy, save Thou me![27]

Henry was increasingly vicious in his old age. There had been no need to execute the Countess, she posed absolutely no threat to him. But when the king decided he wanted somebody gone, his orders were carried out and nobody said otherwise, especially not Bryan.

Whatever he felt he kept to himself, to do otherwise was to countenance his own death and so when Henry went to York to meet with his nephew James V in September Bryan went with him. It was to be an unsuccessful journey for two reasons. Firstly, James didn't show up. Although his mother Margaret, Henry's older sister, pressed him to attend James bore no love for his uncle. He travelled as far as the border but then turned back. Henry was furious but worse was to come.

During the trip, Catherine Howard had had opportunity to sleep with her lover. Unlike Anne who allegedly slept with five men if not more, Catherine was guilty of an affair with Thomas Culpeper. There is some debate over how physical the relationship was. That there was a relationship we are certain but to what heights it had reached we cannot be sure. Catherine had had a relationship with Henry Mannox, her music teacher, prior to 1538 when she moved to the Dowager Duchess of Norfolk's household in Lambeth where she had also had a relationship with Francis Dereham to the point they called each other husband and wife. When her previous behaviour came to light, it signalled the fall of Henry's fifth queen.

Many witnesses were interrogated about the queen. The Dowager Duchess of Norfolk was questioned in December and mentioned Bryan:

She told Sir Francis Brian, coming to her for K. H. (Kath. Howard's) 500 mks., that she would have bonds for the restitution of it if she died before she were married, saying that she heard that Culpeper was in love with her. Has heard since that she "would go abroad to banquet half a mile from her house having a good company with her".[28]

Although Catherine and Bryan were related they do not seem to have been close and Bryan himself was not questioned as he had been over Anne Boleyn's downfall. Culpeper and Dereham were charged with high treason at Guildhall on 1 December 1541 and executed at Tyburn on 10 December 1541. Culpeper was beheaded but Dereham suffered being hanged, drawn and quartered. Catherine Howard was executed on 13 February along with Jane Boleyn, Lady Rochford, at the Tower of London. Bryan did not attend.

Lord Lisle after spending two years in prison was restored to favour. The king told the French ambassador that he 'cannot believe the said Deputy hath erred of malice, but that in those things of which he stands accused he hath proceeded rather by ignorance'.[29] In January 1542 Henry returned to Lisle his collar of the Garter and in March sent him a diamond ring with news of his impending release. He was so excited that his heart failed soon after hearing the news and he was buried in the Chapel Royal of St Peter ad Vincula in the Tower grounds. Bryan had lost one of his closest friends – a man who the king had once said had 'the gentlest heart living'.[30]

And there was more sorrow to come. In October he heard

of his friend Thomas Wyatt's death at Clifton Maybank House in Dorset. Wyatt had been on the way to greet a Spanish envoy who had landed at Falmouth but a 'black pestilence took hold of him'.[31] He fought it off for three days but was not to recover and was laid to rest in Sherborne Abbey at the age of 39.

Life went on for Bryan who was elected to the senior place for Buckinghamshire in parliament this year and continued on with his court duties. In November he received a grant of land in St Albans 'including the two chapels of St. Mary Magdalene and St. Germaynen in St. Alban's, Herts, with certain mills and tithes there'.[32]

Bryan had in fact done well from the dissolution of the monasteries. His grants were numerous and included Ravenstone Priory, Canons Ashby which he sold to Sir John Cope, Repton Priory and Monks Risborough. He was made steward of several other properties including Sulby Abbey. He wrote to Cromwell 'The abbot of Sulbye, whose steward I am, lately came to ask my counsel about surrendering his house. I advised him to go to you and declare his mind, and I beg you to be good lord for his pension'.[33] Cromwell gave the abbot a yearly pension of £50. In London, Bryan was keeper of Chelsea and Canonbury in Islington as well as owning other properties around the city.

And there were more grants to come but issues over one dissolved priory would see him being sued in the Court of Requests.

Markyate Priory had been leased to Humphrey Bourchier, Bryan's cousin. His father John was Lady Margaret Bryan's brother and Bryan's uncle. Humphrey had spent a fortune on turning the priory into his home for him and his wife Elizabeth Bacon. After his death in 1540, Elizabeth married George Ferrers who had studied canon law at Cambridge and was by Leland's account a skilful narrator at the bar. Ferrers had grown up in Cromwell's household and became one of the king's spears. At some time during the period 1541 to 1547, Ferrers, on behalf of his wife who was executrix of Humphrey Bourchier's will, took a case against Sir Francis Bryan. The £200 for the lease of Markyate had been given to Bryan 'in readiness to be paid to the King's use' but three years had passed and the money had gone no further 'to the great deceit of the king'.[34]

Humphrey had been good to Bryan. When he asked to buy abbey goods totalling £81 Humphrey had sold them to him and when Bryan was 'destitute and unprovided of money' he sold the goods on for him and gave him the purchase price. They had both been involved in a transaction with William Epgrave, an embroiderer from London 'in a great sum of money for payment of 100l' which came to the only use of Sir Francis. Humphrey had also lent Bryan divers goods, money and a chain of gold totalling £75 of which he had only paid £50 back. Humphrey then became ill 'by reason of ingratitude' and died £1000 in debt, wanting monies owed by Bryan to go to his wife.[35]

Elizabeth had contacted him and asked for the £200 back. Bryan 'confessed the same' but said the king was happy with his sale of Pondysburne Woods 'which he holdeth in right of his wife' and promised to see the house at Markyate would go to her husband's brethren as per his will. But Ferrers insisted that 'by colour of the pretended purchase'.[36] Bryan still retained the £200 and had not kept his promises, calling on the king to make Bryan answer for the same. There is no extant response from Bryan and the king must have dealt with him privately. After Elizabeth's death however, George Ferrers inherited Markyate.

Bryan had weathered the storm of Henry's latest two unsuccessful marriages and his own relationship with the king. He must have been wondering what was to come with the New Year.

Thomas Wyatt

Chapter Nine

To War with France

1543–1547

Bryan was appointed vice-admiral in January 1543 – because he had 'been vice-admiral before and is experienced in sea matters'[1] – under the lord admiral, John Dudley, who had become Viscount Lisle after the death of his stepfather and 'by the right of his mother'[2] in 1542. Bryan was in his late forties or early fifties by now and had reached a good age for a Tudor noble but his expertise would still be needed.

The previous year had seen the Duke of Norfolk antagonising the Scots with renewed border raids. Henry sent troops towards Scotland when James V retaliated and sent his men across the border. The battle of Solway Moss resulted in few casualties for the English but over 1200 Scottish deaths, many of whom drowned in the River Esk. James V died weeks later leaving his second wife Marie de Guise and young daughter Mary behind.

Henry was anxious that the French were stopped from aiding either the regent, James Hamilton, 2nd Earl of Arran, or Cardinal Beaton, leader of the pro-French party. He ordered a fleet of ships to patrol the east coast. Marie's father Claude de Guise, who was feared might take his daughter and granddaughter back to France, was reported to be victualling his ships at Le Havre and they were to stop them arriving at all costs.

The King takes this apprehension of his ships in the Trade and this passage of Guise into Scotland much to heart, and desires Lisle and Brian to set forth the ten ships already appointed there and as many more as can be furnished in Newcastle and those parts; caring not what charge he is at, but only fearing that they may pass before his fleet is in the Frithe to meet them… Lisle is to write to Arran that he hears how Guise "is coming thither, by mean of the Cardinal, to get the government, child and holds of Scotland into his hands"; and shall also have this news of Guise's coming bruited abroad and signify it to Anguishe (the earl of Angus)… Finally, when it comes to fighting, "you, Master Bryan," will have special regard to the French ship in which Guise himself goes, and in any wise take it.[3]

Bryan's instructions were clear but when he arrived at Newcastle he found only six of his ten ships ready to sail and he reported 'there are more pretty ships here able to serve; but no mariners and no ordinance, and very little powder'.[4]

The Lord Admiral met him at Newcastle and reported that 'Mr. Bryan will set forth with them towards Holy Eland, and wait there for the rest of the navy, in pursuance of the Council's last letters of the 23rd, received yesternight. It is prudent of the King to make his navy strong enough to encounter the Duke of Guise, who will not venture to Scotland without a great "conserve"'.[5]

Bryan patrolled the waters but the Duke of Guise's ships remained elusive although he did capture two French vessels. At the beginning of February his ship the *Elizabeth*, manned by over 100 men, was caught in a storm and there were fears for his safety. But he was soon spotted and Henry issued fresh instructions to detain any French ships.

Suffolk was reporting to the council however that Bryan wasn't exactly following orders:

Enclose a letter to Lisle from Mr. Brian which seems to imply a determination contrary to that agreed upon by Lisle and him. Cannot tell what private instructions Brian may have, but think he will do little good in the Frithe; and that meanwhile the King's subjects and provisions shall be spoiled, for Brian means not to send any ships of war southward, but leave two ships of war which, as he supposes, be setting forth from Lynne to repair to the Foreland

and conduct the provisions.[6]

Bryan reported back to the council on 23 February 1543 but his time as vice-admiral was coming to a close as Henry signed the peace treaty of Greenwich with Scotland. It allowed for the marriage of James V's daughter Mary, soon to be crowned Queen of Scots, to Henry's son Edward, although it would not come to pass and England would continue to be at war with Scotland for the next seven years.

Bryan however was still concerned with naval business and was ordered to send the Lord Admiral 200 mariners for his ships. Dudley was in regular contact with Bryan and sent him a report of the coming of Sir Thomas Wyndham, vice-admiral and navigator, from the West seas:

> *Wyndam says they will do no service where they lie; and, considering that the French pour out ships as they do, the said four ships might well join the others now going to sea; and, together, they will soon "make clean seas."*[7]

There was still much concern about French ships in English waters and the threat they posed. Not only that but Henry wanted the situation in Scotland to be resolved so that he could concentrate on his next invasion of France.

Bryan was gifted more lands in May and June for his service and was back serving the king at court when the king married his last wife Katherine Parr on 12 July 1543. Katherine was the daughter of Sir Thomas Parr, a descendant of Edward III. Bryan had been close to her father, living in his household when young and was friends with her brother.

Katherine had been married to Sir Edward Burgh but two years after his death was proposed to by Lord Latimer of Snape Castle in Yorkshire. By 1543 her husband was unwell and had not long to live. She hoped to marry Sir Thomas Seymour, brother of

Henry's third wife, but it was not to be. The king wanted her and what the king wanted he inevitably got but Katherine had no ambition to become the next Queen of England. Henry by now had grown 'very stout and daily growing heavier, he seems very old and grey...'[8] but she would prove to be a caring and dutiful wife. Just what Henry needed.

Sir Thomas Wriothesley, Lord Chancellor, wrote 'the king's majesty was married on Thursday last to my lady Latimer, a woman, in my judgement, for virtue, wisdom and gentleness most meet for his highness; and sure I am his majesty had never a wife more agreeable to his heart than she is'.[9]

While the king settled into married life once again, Bryan was sent as ambassador to Charles V, accompanied by Henry Howard, the Earl of Surrey, in October 1543. Before he left he visited the Spanish ambassador, Eustace Chapuys, in London, to inform him of his mission including that 'The King of England wishes to know before hand what is to be done next year against the common enemy, and when and at what point of their frontier the French are to be assailed, so that he himself may prepare and make the necessary provision for the undertaking'.[10] Chapuys thought highly of Bryan writing to Antoine Perrenot de Granvelle, advisor to Charles V, 'the friendship which unites us, and the many obligations under which I am to him, compel me to request and beg Your Lordship to show him all possible favor'.[11]

Charles V had been on campaign taking back parts of the Low Countries, including those ruled by Anne of Cleves' brother, William. The capital of Juliers, Duren, had been taken with 'the garrison, and most of the inhabitants, being put to the sword'.[12] In September the duke signed the treaty of Venlo with the emperor. He gave up Guelders and Zutphen but Charles allowed him to keep Juliers and what little was left of it.

Henry wanted to ensure Charles V would stay true to the Anglo-Imperial treaty they had signed earlier in the year with a commitment to invade France within two years, each providing

20,000 foot and 5000 horse. On 24 October Bryan met with the emperor near Landrecy to congratulate him on his recent victory and to be assured of his loyalty.

The Privy Council sent on Henry's instructions:

The King requires him to declare to the Emperor that, considering how events, whether prosperous or adverse, concern them both, he has studied how best to proceed against the common enemy; and thinks that, as the French king has been at importable charges this year and will be unable to re-assemble such forces next year, the Emperor should defer joining battle with him at present, unless at manifest advantage or if unable in honor to avoid it. The King expects that, next year, he on the one side and the Emperor on the other will compel the enemy, deprived of the friends and forces he now has, to endure such loss as will never be recovered. He, however, remits the whole to the Emperor's experience and wisdom, who is near enough to his enemy to see what honor and advantage can be gained without loss.[13]

Bryan and the Earl of Surrey joined Sir John Wallop, captain of Guînes since 1541, and his men at Landrecy on 4 November for a council of war with Charles V. Wallop had led 6000 men there in July to take the town from the French in a joint effort with Charles V's troops. Francis I's army was advancing diverting their attention from the siege but just as they turned their attention towards him, the French army quietly slipped away at night. They chased after the French soldiers but to no avail and it was decided to send the men back to England.

The emperor asked Bryan if he would be staying longer with the army and he thought not. He had heard that the Duke of Lorraine was on his way to see the emperor to sue for peace and concerned that Charles might go back on their treaty he stayed.

Bryan wrote to Henry on 19 November:

On Saturday, the 17th, the duke of Lorraine and his son arrived at Vallencia, with 200 horse; and, after dinner, had access to the Emperor and the Queen... (Lorraine) who, after wearying the Emperor with praises, pointed out that if the Emperor and French king continued at war, the Turk would overcome Christendom, and that the Germans were not yet in order; and after swearing, with his hand on his breast, that he "had no commission from none alive" (an oath learnt, as Granvelle said, in France, where "so they swear when they lie most"), said that Barbarosse should be sent out of France when the Emperor would, and desired a peace or else some truce. The Emperor replied, that, as to peace, since he had no commission it would be waste of wind to answer him, and, as for Barbarosse, he "was not a counsel for his coming" nor would "meddle with his going," thinking his abode the more charge to his enemy; and that he was in league with the King of England, without whom he would enterprise nothing... The Emperor then asked Brian if Granvelle had told him touching the duke of Lorrayne, and said "'Heard ye ever a stranger sort of coming?' 'Sir,' quod I, 'ye saw that at this present he had assembled all the power that he could make in all his realm and elsewhere to fight against you, and yet durst not tarry it. How will he do the next year when my master shall be of as great power of his own partie?' 'Mary,' quod th'Emperor, 'I trust, undone.' 'Now, Sir,' quod I, 'the sticking to you of a faithful friend makes your enemy to shrink.' 'And I,' quod he, 'never to fail my friend again.'" Surrey and Brian then went to the Queen, whom they found sitting before a fire, playing at cards with the duke of Lorraine. While Surrey spoke with the Queen, Brian saluted the Duke, who sat, as he is lame, and asked Brian, for their old acquaintance in France, to drink with him before he departed. The Queen then called Brian, "saying, 'Mons. Ambassador, heard you ever of so lean a message?' 'Madame,' quod I, 'if the broth be no fatter it is not worthy the supping.' With that she laughed; so we departed."... Was afterwards assured that Lorraine comes for peace, but the Emperor will do nothing without Henry.[14]

Bryan was recalled at the end of November when Dr Nicholas Wotton, Dean of Canterbury and a seasoned diplomat, was sent in his place. Wotton had arrived by 5 December when he, Bryan and Bonner, bishop of London, reported to Henry:

> *The Emperor replied that it was natural for every man to desire to return to his own country, and therefore he could not but be content that Brian and Bonner should return; that Wotton was welcome; that his provision of ships had been hindered by other affairs and by misfortune at sea, but he had given order for its amendment; and that, as for the Duke of Loreyne, Henry's opinion was true, and also a prisoner coming out of France had affirmed that the Cardinal of Liningcourt ("whom he called the Cardinal of Lorraine's Cardinal") had expressed a wish for peace, but the French were mad to go about to deceive him always with the same means instead of trying some new craft. Brian thereupon showed how the French sought peace with Henry also; who, however, intended to make preparation against next year, and desired the Emperor to do the like. The Emperor approved this, and said he would send the Viceroy of Sicily to Henry, with power to conclude all things pertaining thereto; and willed them to repair to Mons. Granvell, the Viceroy and Mons. de Prate. Bonner and Brian then took leave; and, according to the Emperor's command, sent to Granvell, who replied "that it could not be for that day." Brian then took Mons. de Herbes and other gentlemen to his lodging to dinner...*[15]

Bryan was back in England at the end of December and the New Year saw Henry gearing up for war with the French. Bryan raised 200 men to join the army of 10,000 that would serve under the Duke of Norfolk to besiege the medieval walled port town of Montreuil, forty miles south of Calais

They were joined by the Count of Duren and his Flemish soldiers who knew the lay of the country better, but Norfolk was loath to trust him reporting, 'We might have been at Montreuil three or four days past but we, knowing no part of the country, nor having no guides but such as they gave us, have been brought such ways as we think never army passed, up and down the hills, through hedges, woods and marshes, and all to cause us to lodge upon the French grounds, saving their own friends'.[16]

When they arrived at Montreuil through torrential rain, they found it difficult to take up an offensive position due to the flat land surrounding it which made them easy targets for the French. 'None of us ever saw so evil a town to make approach unto'.[17]

Norfolk, now in his seventies, began a barrage of correspondence to complain to the Privy Council of the shortages his army faced. His soldiers were on rations but hoarding what they could find. They ran out of beer and stripped the countryside around Montreuil of grain and livestock.

Montreuil was well defended by its walls and cannon and the siege dragged on. Meanwhile Henry had arrived at Boulogne in July 1544 to meet with the duke of Suffolk, in command of the King's army. Henry ignored Norfolk's pleas for reinforcements and concentrated on taking Boulogne. A soldier at Montreuil, Elis Gruffydd, cynically wrote in his journal 'the King did not intend to capture Montreuil but only set them to lie there so that he and his host might take their ease and sleep more easily in their beds in the camp around Boulogne'.[18] Bryan was sent to Henry at Boulogne to explain the situation but the king would not accept defeat at Montreuil or give the order for them to retreat and sent him back again.

Boulogne lay in two parts, lower and upper. After heavy bombardment, the lower section fell with ease but the upper and its castle took a debilitating amount of time. To breach the castle, tunnels were dug under its stone foundations and Boulogne surrendered on 18 September, to Henry's delight and his troops' relief. 'And so... the duke of Suffolke rode into Bullein, to who in the kynges name, they deliuered the keyes of the toune'.[19]

Henry celebrated his triumph until he heard that Charles V

had signed a treaty with the French thus removing his troops from the area. At Montreuil the Dutch contingency left Norfolk and Bryan to it on hearing the news.

The siege at Boulogne had been victorious but the siege at Montreuil had stagnated. The earl of Surrey, Norfolk's son and Marshal of the Field, had managed to capture some small towns and found a herd of cattle to the delight of the soldiers but with no reinforcements they were fighting a losing battle.

Norfolk and Bryan were now in difficulty as the French began to close in around them and cut off their supplies. Francis I ordered his son, the Dauphin Henri, to relieve the town with 50,000 men under his command. Finally Henry ordered a retreat. On 28 September they headed for Boulogne and arrived two days later.

Henry and Norfolk made their way back to England but Bryan stayed on in Boulogne until April 1545 with a small garrison of 4000 men initially under Lord Lisle's command, but when he was recalled back to sea, Lord Poynings took over. The rest of the army, those that had survived, straggled back to their homes but many were sick and dying.

The soldiers coming from Calais and Boulogne were dying along the road from Dover to London and along the roads from London to every quarter of the Kingdom while trying to go to their homes. After they had come home, those who were well fell sick and those who were sick got worse and from this sickness and feebleness and pest they died in every part of England, mostly the people who had been in the camps at Montreuil among whom both before and after there was the greatest pest that ever was among people.[20]

Henry ordered that the town be repaired and its shattered walls be rebuilt but the labourers fared no better than the soldiers had done. Twelve hundred men were sent over to work in Boulogne and by June only 300 were left.

Bryan managed to retain his health despite being surrounded by disease and deprivation but the threat of war with Scotland and France remained and on Bryan's return he and other nobles were commissioned to raise funds which he did for Bedfordshire. The Lord Admiral, John Dudley, was again amassing a sea fleet but instead of taking the post of vice-admiral again Bryan was commissioned to review the defences of the south coast with Sir John Russell, 1st Earl of Bedford and Lord Privy Seal, who he had fought alongside at Montreuil, seeing all the coast from 'beyond the Mounte and set order for their defence'. Russell wrote:

Begs that Mr. Bryan, who, if Russell should be sick, is the meetest man here to do the affairs of this country, may in future put his hand to such letters as Russell sends to the King and Council.[21]

It was whilst they were travelling through Dorset and Cornwall making sure that defences were in place that they heard of the sinking of the *Mary Rose*, Henry's famous warship under the command of Sir George Carew. Two hundred French ships carrying 30,000 men and the English navy clashed in July. The English were vastly outnumbered with only eighty ships and around 12,000 men but managed to scatter the French fleet in the Solent. There are several theories as to why the *Mary Rose* sunk, the most probable being that with her gunports open she turned suddenly and water flooded into the ship. Although the French landed on the Isle of Wight and Seaford in Sussex they were repelled. The French captain unable to revictual his ships and with sickness amongst the crew returned to France. The threat of invasion was thwarted but the loss of the *Mary Rose* and nearly all of her 400-strong crew was a bitter blow.

In the days that followed William Paget and Charles Brandon tried to organise a recovery mission but they were unable to see the ship raised and only some rigging and guns were retrieved. The Duke of Suffolk in fact was ailing and the king's closest companion died in August at Guildford of unknown causes.

Bryan may have gone up to Windsor for his funeral at St George's Chapel but he was still busy with Russell investigating the unauthorised searches of priest's houses in Somerset and Dorset. They had been contacted by the sheriff in Sherbourne whose men had been conducting the searches, because he was not clear on who had sent such instructions. The order had not come from the Privy Council and Russell put a stop to the searches whilst Bryan travelled to Bridgewater where it seemed as if the threat of a French invasion had just caused people to panic.

Russell reported, 'Searching of priests has caused no small stir in Dorset and Somersetshire. Being bruited as commanded by the King (and yet no commission shown) the matter passed from constable to constable and from tithing man to tithing man, who, being ignorant people, took no advice of justices or gentlemen and ran as headlong a search as Russell ever heard of. Has taken order to prevent it in this shire and stop it in Dorset and Somerset...'[22]

There was a celebration held for Bryan this year when he was given the freedom of the city of London. An honour given by the guilds, it may have been in relation to his association with the Goldsmiths Company of which he was a gentleman member.

England was still gearing up for war with France in 1546 but lack of funds and with Henry now an aging king meant hostilities would cease and in June a peace treaty was signed. In August the French Admiral Claude d'Annebault and his ambassadors visited England for its ratification. Bryan did not play a principal role in greeting them but did attend the dinner held in their honour.

The queen graciously welcomed their guests but Katherine had very nearly not been there. Katherine was known for her reformist views and this had led to a quarrel with her husband over religion. It had gone so far that Henry had ordered her arrest but Katherine knew she was in danger and when the king led her into another discussion that would have seen her damned in his eyes she passively told her husband, 'Since, therefore, that God hath appointed such a natural difference between man and woman, and your Majesty being so excellent in gifts and ornaments of wisdom, and I a silly poor woman, so much inferior in all respects of nature unto you, how then cometh it now to pass that your Majesty, in such diffuse causes of religion, will seem to require my judgment? which when I have uttered and said what I can, yet must I, and will I, refer my judgment in this, and in all other cases, to your Majesty's wisdom, as my only anchor, supreme head and governor here in earth, next under God, to lean unto'.[23]

Katherine told him she had only been debating religion with him as way to take his mind off the pain in his ulcerated leg. Henry replied 'Is it even so, sweetheart? And tended your arguments to no worse end? Then perfect friends we are now again, as ever at any time heretofore'.[24] The queen had saved herself but Wriothesley had already been instructed to arrest her the following day.

When Katherine was out walking with the king in his privy garden, the Lord Chancellor approached her surrounded by forty guards. Henry shouted 'Knave! Arrant knave, beast! And fool!' The he commanded Wriotheseley 'presently to avaunt out of his presence. Which words, although they were uttered somewhat low, yet were they so vehemently whispered out by the king, that the queen did easily, with her ladies aforesaid, overhear them; which had been not a little to her comfort, if she had known at that time the whole cause of his coming, as perfectly as after she knew it'.[25] It was a narrow escape but Katherine kept her head.

One who was not so lucky was Bryan's friend, kinsman and fellow poet, Henry Howard, Earl of Surrey. He was arrested in December and his father Thomas Howard, 3rd Duke of Norfolk, was also imprisoned. Surrey was led through the streets of

London to the Tower 'the crowd offered nothing but loud sympathy, saying aloud that it was a pity to put so fair a knight in the Tower'.[26]

On 13 January Surrey was charged with treason as 'he had on 7 October 1546 at Kenninghall displayed in his own heraldry the royal arms and insignia, with three labels silver, thereby threatening the king's title to the throne and the prince's inheritance'. [27]

Surrey pleaded not guilty. 'For eight hours, Surrey stood up against all attacks, and he more than once succeeded in covering his accusers in confusion, most of whom almost certainly knew less about the rules of heraldry than he'.[28]

He was beheaded on Tower Hill on 19 January 1547. Bryan had shared the position of cupbearer with Surrey and he inherited his gown of gold. The Duke of Norfolk, although confessing to offending the king, stayed in the Tower until his release in Mary I's reign. He talked of Bryan in his testimony.

Also I was asked whether I was privy to a letter from my Lord of Winchester and Sir Henry Knevet "of an overture made by Grandvile to them for a way to be taken between his Majesty and the Bishop of Rome, and that the said letter should have come to his Majesty to Dover, I being then with him?" I was never at Dover with his Majesty "since my Lord of Richmond died, but at that time, of whose death word came to Syttyngborne," and I never heard of such overture. I remember that when Sir Francis Bryan was sick and like to die it was said in the Council ' that my Lord of Winchester should have said he could devise a way how the King's Majesty might save all things upright with the said Bishop of Rome, and his Highness' honor saved"; and that one was sent to Sir Francis to know if he had ever heard the Bishop so speak, which he denied. It was Sir Ralph Sadeler who was sent. I never heard of such an overture by Grandvile, nor ever communed with any man concerning any other matter than this of the Bp. of Winchester.[29]

All the king's men were falling away and the king himself had not long to follow.

Henry VIII died at Whitehall on 28 January. There is no record of Bryan being at his side although Sander quoted Henry as saying, 'Bryan we have lost all'[30] before he passed away. Initially his death was kept a secret but on 31 January Lord Chancellor Wriothesley made the announcement to parliament through a stream of tears. Edward VI was declared king the same day.

Henry's body began its journey in a gilded chariot pulled by eight horses to St George's Chapel in Windsor on 14 February. The roads from Westminster to Windsor had been made ready to allow the four mile long procession to pass. On route, it stopped at Syon Abbey for the night where it is said that his coffin burst open and dogs gruesomely licked at his remains.

Once the coffin was repaired, Henry continued on his journey to his final resting place alongside the wife he had loved the most, the wife that had given him his only legitimate son, Jane Seymour. King Henry was buried on 16 February in St George's Chapel at Windsor Castle, with none of his family present apart from his sixth wife Katherine who watched from the privacy of the Queen's Closet. After masses were said and Henry's coat of arms, helmet, shield and sword were placed reverentially on the altar, the service was ended with the proclamation 'Le roi est mort! Vive le roi!'

Bryan attended his funeral as master of the henchmen. He had lost the man whose service he had stayed in and survived. Now it was to be seen what would be in store for them all with a new reign.

The Tomb of Katherine Parr

Chapter Ten

Final Days in Ireland

1547–1550

Edward VI was crowned on 20 February 1547. Henry's ultimate wish had come true and his son would now rule after him – at least for the next six years. Bryan stayed loyal to the new king and in May was awarded the keepership of six royal parks in Bedfordshire for life. His landed wealth was now assessed at £888, a rise of £488 since 1527.

However he was not elected for Edward's first parliament in August. The Lord Protector, Edward Seymour, the late Queen Jane's brother, was given the power to choose the new Privy Council and Bryan would not be as close to the new king as he had been to the old. Times had changed and with it the men in power.

Bryan was in his fifties now but his skills were still needed and in September he was called on to join the Lord Protector in his campaign against Scotland 'to win not a battle alone but a country'.[1] England had hoped for a peaceful solution by proposing a marriage between the infant Mary Queen of Scots and Edward VI but Scotland's regent Marie de Guise wished her daughter to marry the dauphin of France and was backed by 4000 French soldiers, sent over from France's new king, Henry II, who had succeeded after the death of his father Francis I in March. The Scottish force was amassing close to the border and Bryan was given command of 2000 light horse. With over 10,000 soldiers they made their way from Berwick towards Edinburgh clashing with Scottish and French troops.

At Musselburgh the English encountered the Scottish army who were trying to take a prominent position at a high ridge overlooking the town. Bryan urged his men forward and fiercely fought them back, forcing their retreat but a more violent confrontation was to come.

On 10 September the Battle of Pinkie Cleugh was a victory for the English with around 10,000 Scots killed. William Patten described the carnage:

Soon after this notable strewing of their footmen's weapons, began a pitiful sight of the dead corpses lying dispersed abroad, some their legs off, some but houghed, and left lying half-dead, some thrust quite through the body, others the arms cut off, diverse their necks half asunder, many their heads cloven, of sundry the brains pasht out, some others again their heads quite off, with other many kinds of killing. After that and further in chase, all for the most part killed either in the head or in the neck, for our horsemen could not well reach the lower with their swords. And thus with blood and slaughter of the enemy, this chase was continued five miles in length westward from the place of their standing, which was in the fallow fields of Inveresk until Edinburgh Park and well nigh to the gates of the town itself and unto Leith, and in breadth nigh 4 miles, from the Firth sands up toward Dalkeith southward. In all which space, the dead bodies lay as thick as a man may note cattle grazing in a full replenished pasture. The river ran all red with blood, so that in the same chase were counted, as well by some of our men that somewhat diligently did mark it as by some of them taken prisoners, that very much did lament it, to have been slain about 14 thousand. In all this compass of ground what with weapons, arms, hands, legs, heads, blood and dead bodies, their flight might have been easily tracked to every of their three refuges. And for the smallness of our number and the shortness of the time (which was scant five hours, from one to well nigh six) the mortality was so great, as it was thought, the like aforetime not to have been seen... [2]

It was a vicious and bloody battle. The strictly Protestant Edward

VI was delighted at their victory and on hearing that amongst the slain were Catholic priests he wrote to Seymour, 'For I hope that they will be conquered and routed, and at last, that all the ringleaders of this tumult and mischief are going out of the world. However, there is no doubt we shall conquer; for we fight for the cause of God, they for that of the pope'.[3] Scotland would be garrisoned with English soldiers but by 1549 they would be withdrawn and Mary Queen of Scots would marry the dauphin and not Edward.

Bryan was made knight-banneret in 1547 for his role in the campaign, the highest office obtainable in the field but it would signal an end to his soldiering days. Bryan was able to return home to Woburn from where he organised timber to be taken to Brogborough Park, north of his residence, to build a house for the king's intended visit.

He had certainly had more time now he wasn't required at court and in 1548 his anonymous translation of Antonio de Guevara's *A Dispraise of the Life of the Courtier* was published. Antonio de Guevara was a bishop, preacher and chronicler at the court of Charles V. Bryan's uncle Lord Berners had introduced him to Guevara's work and had translated *The Golden Book of Marcius Aurelius* himself. Whilst Berners' translation was based on the writings of the Roman emperor, Bryan's book looked at the pleasures of country life as opposed to the struggles of life at court which was full of 'gentlemen so rooted in vengeance and hatred that by no means, request nor gentleness a man may direct them from their evil intents'. He dedicated his translation to William Parr, Marquis of Northampton, brother to the dowager queen Katherine, whose father had welcomed Bryan into his household as a child. Bryan wrote in the dedication that it was partly due to Parr's urging that he had decided to translate the work. Parr had also encouraged his sister, the queen, to write *The Lamentation of a Sinner* which had been published the previous year.

Bryan had long been a patron of the arts. The scholar Florens Volusenus dedicated his commentary to Psalms 51 to him in 1531 and in 1547 Robert Whittington would dedicate his translation of a collection of moral sayings *A frutefull work of Lucius Anneus Senecae called the myrrour or glasse of maners* to him. Bryan was known as a poet yet none of his works are extant. Although 'The Proverbes of Salmon' may have been his:

The proverbes of Salmon do playnly declare
That wysdome ys the vessell that longest will endure...
When thowe spekest let men marvell at thy shamefacenes
When thow spekest not let them wondre at thy sobernes.
Withe leavinge honour to women I ende, quod Bryan.[4]

And he is also thought to have been co-author with Henry Howard, earl of Surrey, and Thomas Wyatt for their *Tottel's Miscellany of English Poetry*. The Elizabethan poet Michael Drayton definitely thought so and would describe in his own poem:

When after those, foure ages very neare,
They with the Muses which conuersed, were
That Princely Surrey, early in the time
Of the Eight Henry, who was then the prime
Of Englands noble youth; with him there came
Wyat; with reuerence whom we still doe name
Amongst our Poets, Brian had a share,
With the two former, which accompted are
That times best makers, and the authors were
Of those small poems, which the title beare,
Of songs and sonnets, wherein of they hit
On many dainty passages of wit.[5]

And further mentioned him in another poem in *England's Heroical Epistles* published in 1695 thus:

And sacred Bryan, (whom the Muses kept
And in his Cradle rockt him whilst he slept)
In sacred Verses (most divinely pen'd)
Upon thy prayses ever shall attend.[6]

Francis Meres writing in *Palladis Tamia, Wits Treasury* in 1598 also had Bryan in a list of poets 'so these are the most passionate among us to bewail and bemoan the perplexities of love, Henry Howard, Earl of Surrey, Sir Thomas Wyatt the elder, Sir Francis Bryan, Sir Philip Sidney, Sir Walter Raleigh, Sir Edward Dyer, Spenser, Daniel, Drayton, Shakespeare, Whetstone, Gascoigne, Samuel Page'.[7] It is such a shame that a man notorious for being a rake left behind none of his love poems. They may have helped to illuminate his next marriage.

Bryan's friend Thomas Wyatt had advised him to marry a wealthy widow after his first wife Philippa died sometime after 1542. Urged on by the Privy Council he now married Joan Butler, dowager countess of Ormond, and daughter of James FitzGerald, 10th Earl of Desmond, around August 1548.

Joan had been married to James Butler, the 9th Earl of Ormond and 2nd Earl of Ossory, once considered a possible husband for Anne Boleyn. Bryan had met him several times as he served in the French campaign of 1513, accompanied himself and Wolsey to France in 1521 and had served Henry VIII in London for six years before returning to Ireland.

In 1546 Henry had recalled Butler and Sir Anthony St Leger, Lord Deputy of Ireland, to answer for their continuous feud. St Leger is said to have remarked that only one of them would survive the investigation which turned out to be true.

On 17 October Butler and his household were invited to dine with the 1st Duke of Northumberland at Ely Palace in Holborn. The earl, his steward, James Whyte, and sixteen of his household were poisoned but no investigation was made into their deaths. The finger of suspicion was pointed at St Leger but by this point they had made up their differences and Butler had appointed him as supervisor of his will.

His wife Joan was not with him at the time but was later called to England to prevent her from marrying Gerald FitzGerald, one of the Desmond clan, who had no love for English authority and who they feared would rule in her son's stead as he had not yet reached his majority.

Upon the late Erle of Ormond's dethe it was suspected as thing wolde happed indead, that the Countess of ormonde intended to marry therle of Desmonds sonne and heir, whereby therle of Ormonde being not in age he sholde be a mean to make all his rule incyvill and yrishe: for avoiding she was sent for into Inglande and bestowed as she was.[8]

Bryan was convinced to make an alliance with the widowed Joan for the sake of the crown. She was definitely unhappy with the match saying, 'While I was a widow and not married [to] an Englishman, I defended and kept my own, or at the least, no man went about to defeat me of my right. Well is the woman unmarried; I am bade to hold my peace, and my husband shall have answer made unto him.'[9]

Perhaps to thank him for his service Bryan was granted the bishops palace at Norwich and tenancy of parts of Blackfriars in London including the hall and previous lodgings of the friars including a storehouse, a larderhouse, a gallery and rooms of a parlour, a great chamber, a great dining chamber (probably the hall) and two gardens.

In September, 'Sr Francis Brian, hath taken his leve and is now sogeorning in the country aboute som of his own possessions wth my lady his wife and it is bruted that they entend to be at Chester'. From there they travelled on to Dublin in October where Lord Deputy Bellingham had left provisions of a 'half tune wyne, tune beyre, and six fatt mertes to his welcum'[10] at his house in Kilmainham.

Although Sir Edward Bellingham, Lord Deputy of Ireland since April 1548, and Sir John Alen, Lord Chancellor of Ireland, didn't want him there. Alen thought he was an expensive man to have around costing the king around £40,000. He said 'he favoured Sir Edward Bellyngham's toe more than Sir Francis Bryan's body'.[11] But Bryan assumed his position on the Irish Council with responsibility for Tipperary and Kilkenny in lieu of Joan's son, Thomas Butler, 10th Earl of Ormond and 3rd Earl of Ossory, a ward of the crown, who had been created a knight of the bath at Edward VI's christening and had grown up with the king. Bryan would also take the role of lord marshal in command of the royal forces in January 1549.

Brigden describes how 'through his marriage Bryan wielded Ormond authority in south Leinster, controlling the estates of Thomas Butler, tenth earl of Ormond, in his minority and a private army of gallowglasses in Co. Kilkenny'.[12] One John Issam contacted the Irish Council as he was not happy the Bryan's had gallowglasses – mercenary soldiers – but they had long been a part of the Ormond's army and had served Henry VIII in his Scottish campaign.

Joan also had her dealings with Bellingham, sharing control over her son's estates with him. Their arguments prompted the lord deputy to contact the Privy Council to underline his authority. And Joan was not happy with Bryan's role either. She complained she would rather 'go live upon my own inheritance under my Lord of Desmond and I know he will defend me'.[13] She railed against Bellingham and the council in front of the constable of Carlow Castle who reported that Bryan 'spoke nothing but that which sounded to your lordship's (Bellingham's) honour and gave his wife sweet words'.[14] He also reprimanded her over her stand against another Irish family, the Ryans:

Certain Irishmen of the Ryans came to my Lady of Ormond at

Callan, and there would have made estate of some land to her and her children. Cowley declared that it would be evil taken if they should now cloke Irishmen's lands against the King, when he was ready to set his foot there. Sir Francis Bryan took it in good part, and much reproved my Lady therein. He said he "wolde not borrowe of the lawe as my Lorde of Ormond did."[15]

One William Cantwell who was reporting to Lord Bellingham obviously felt that neither of the Bryan's had any love for the deputy. He wrote on 4 October 1549:

Since his departure from his Lordship he has taken divers persons, for which he receives much malice from the Lord Marshal and his wife. Trusts he shall do the King and his Lordship such service as shall be acceptable. At Kilkenny there is a common saying among the people, and especially among the servants of the Lord Marshal, that the Lord Deputy should shortly repair to England; with many other false sayings. The Lord Protector's servant is riding with the Lord Marshal to Waterford, and will be at Dublin next Thursday... Certifies his Lordship that the Baron of Upper Ossory's servant is "greatest in talk and communication" with the Lord Marshal; in times past they were "most enemies" now they are "most friends".[16]

A few days later Cantwell was reporting more of the same but he felt a rebellion was gathering whereby the Baron of Upper Ossory would 'drive the King's friends out of the realm' when Bellingham returned to England. He did not think that Bryan knew of their plans but felt his wife did as she was going to meet with the Baron in the next ten days 'for what cause he knows not; but he perceives that they are now great friends who were before this open enemies' and still he was suffering from 'great ill-will from the lady Ormond for doing his duty'.[17]

Sometimes however Bryan and his wife could be in agreement as when they granted James White of Clonmel and Nicholas

Brown a lease to the village of Lawleston and permission for Sir William Whelan to make a timber castle at Lysterlyng in Co. Kilkenny.

On 27 December 1549 Bryan was appointed lord justice in Ireland when Bellingham left. He was sent to fortify coastal ports in Munster and set out for Tipperary 'to defend it against the incursions of O'Carroll'[18] who had burnt the castle and town of Nenagh. He suddenly became ill on 2 February 1550 at Clonmel.

Richard Scudamore reported:

Sir Francis Bryan is dead in Ireland, and it is said he died easily, sitting at a table leaning on his elbow, none perceiving any likelihood of death in him. He said these words 'I pray you, let me be buried amongst the good fellows of Waterford which were good drinkers', and upon those words immediately died. God send all Christian men better departure.[19]

An autopsy found no physical reason for his death although there were rumours that his wife had had him poisoned. The author Fuller has commented, 'It is interesting to note that not only did her first husband die unpleasantly, Sir Francis Bryan died of unknown causes while it is said, Joan was seeing Gerald FitzJames, the Rebel Earl who would'.[20] She would in fact marry him after Bryan's death.

But Chancellor Alen did not suspect foul play writing 'Myself lyeing in his house, and being then wt him; and where it had been reported that he should dye of a purgac'on it is not true; for he wolde by no meanes be p'suaded to take any medicine. Alen had been at the autopsy and curiously reported that Bryan had in fact died of grief 'but whereof, so ever he died, he dep'ted very godly'.[21]

Bryan was buried, as he had asked, with full honours at the cathedral church of the Blessed Trinity in Waterford which was rebuilt in 1793 and where nothing remains to signify his resting place. It seems that Joan argued with her kinswoman Lady Katherine Butler whilst there as 'a displeasure arose betwixed these two ladies'[22] which Chancellor Alen muted.

If a will had been found we may have known more about his descendants. There is talk of an illegitimate son arriving in London with a dispatch from the French admiral in 1548 'who has arrived safe and sound and sent with one of Selve's people to London, from which he has left again to go find his father'.[23]

Some believe that Philippa, his first wife, had had a son Edmund and that his second wife Joan had also born a child Francis but no evidence exists for any of Bryan's supposed legitimate children. By the time of her marriage to Bryan, Joan was in her thirties at least and had had seven sons by her first husband. Her childbearing days may well have been over but to many Francis Bryan is one of their ancestors.

Bryan had lived to serve his king. He had been a sailor, a soldier, a diplomat, a poet, and a friend but he had never risen quite as high and far as others even though 'for a time he was considered the emerging favorite, but he could not support his position. He loved drinking and had a talent for mistruth.'[24]

He had survived where many others hadn't. He was known for his familiarity with the king and perhaps this saved him. Henry knew Bryan would tell him how it was in no uncertain terms and he was clever enough to make sure his loyalty was rarely ever in question. His life had not been plain sailing and there had been close calls but Bryan had adapted to the changes that occurred during his king's reign and remains his most notorious ambassador.

Appendix One

Sir Francis Bryan's Religion

It has been difficult to pinpoint Sir Francis Bryan's religious tendencies. Many of his friends were conservative in their leanings as he also appears to have been. Lisle was Catholic as was the Duke of Norfolk and Stephen Gardiner, fellow diplomat and later Mary I's Lord Chancellor. Bryan dined often with Dr John Bell, archdeacon of Gloucester, Dr Richard Wolman, archdeacon of Sudbury and Dr William Knight, archdeacon of Richmond and later bishop of Bath and Wells, more of Mary's supporters.

The bishop of Woburn who died for his beliefs 'extolled the traditions of the old fathers of the Church Catholic'[1] in Bryan's company and had testified that Bryan had a copy of the newly translated English Bible in his bedchamber. When he commented that it was not well interpreted in many places Bryan replied:

Interpretors most sometimes folowe the letter and some the sence, and with that he opened agayn the boke and torned to the words in luke of the consecration of the most blissed body and blode of criste and red the same and asked me (the abbot) howe I lyke that.[2]

In July a spy when questioned said he was Bryan's man and he had papers on him that were for the pope and against Luther. Sir Francis Englefield, a supporter of the Princess Mary, tells of a story of how Bryan chided a Lutheran woman at court. The lady had showed her dislike for Henry VIII's Ten Articles and the king's supremacy. Bryan told her '...if we must have devices in religion, I had rather have them from a king, than from the knave ... Friar Martin, who not yet twenty years ago was deviser of your new religion, and behaved himself so lewdly in answering his Majesty,' referring to Martin Luther's attack on the king and his defence of the seven sacraments. Bryan said 'I would rather for my part stick to the devising of a king that has majesty in him than to a thousand of Luther's companions put together'.[3]

But during Anne Boleyn's ascendancy, he seems to have shown support for the reformation as to retain the king's favour he had to do. Henry's break with Rome signalled such a change that caught many between following their king and following their faith. Part of Bryan's success at court was because he changed with the times, adapted to the will of his sovereign and followed the consensus. He defended Norfolk against accusations of popery and dined with Goodrich, a staunch supporter of Henry's divorce.

Brigden posits that Bryan had a knowledge of scripture as Wyatt's poem to his friend points to a secret message contained within the Book of Ecclesiasticus. Wyatt was himself in favour of reform and known for his evangelical views.

Nicolas Sander, author of the *Rise and Growth of the Anglican Schism*, tells us that when Henry was dying he supposedly told Bryan, 'We have lost all,' referring to the rise of Protestantism, but there is no record of Bryan being at the king's deathbed and he was not mentioned in Henry's will.

Did Bryan then just go along with the changes in religion having no particular preference? Or was there something else going on?

Whilst undertaking the research for this book I found mention of Sir Francis Bryan as being of the Rosicrucian order or the Ancient Mystical Order of the Rose Cross. Although the organisation's roots are much older, the early 1600s saw the publication of three manifestos that renewed interest in this branch of esoteric wisdom. They told the story of Christian Rosenkreuz, a figure of legend as the founder of the order, who travelled to the Middle East and North Africa, to search for hidden knowledge and secret learning.

On a list, which I have been unable to trace or verify, which some authors quote, Sir Francis Bryan precedes Dr John Dee, Elizabeth I's physician and astrologer, as being Grand Master of the Order. Dee certainly studied mysticism and religion. His library contained over 4000 books on a wide variety of topics. His own book, the *Monas Hieroglyphica*, is a study in esoteric symbolism which was later used in Rosicrucian writings.

Stephen Dudley, a current member of the order says 'The hard evidence for a Rosicrucian "movement" thus comes a little late for Bryan. Sir Francis cannot have been Grand Master, but it is possible that he moved in the sort of circles of erudition and mysticism, and why should he not have been a philosopher himself?'

Bryan's religious beliefs are unclear. He certainly towed the line and did as his king wished but he also examined scripture as the Bishop of Woburn testified at his trial. And he may have been involved in much more...

References

Chapter One: The Making of a Courtier

1. Bryan, *A dispraise of the life of a courtier*
2. Vergil, *Anglica Historia*
3. *Letters and Papers, Foreign and Domestic, Henry VIII*
4. BL, Cotton MS, Caligula D VI, f.149
5. *CSP Spain*
6. Weir, *The Lady in the Tower*
7. Hall, *Hall's Chronicle: Containing the history of England*
8. *CSP Spain*
9. Hall, *Hall's Chronicle: Containing the history of England*
10. *Letters and Papers, Foreign and Domestic, Henry VIII*
11. Weir, *Henry VIII: King and Court*
12. *CSP Venice*
13. Hall, *Hall's Chronicle: Containing the history of England*
14. Ibid.
15. Ibid.
16. *Letters and Papers, Foreign and Domestic, Henry VIII*
17. *CSP Venice*
18. *Letters and Papers, Foreign and Domestic, Henry VIII*
19. Hall, *Hall's Chronicle: Containing the history of England*
20. Ibid.
21. *Letters and Papers, Foreign and Domestic, Henry VIII*
22. Ibid.

Chapter Two: To France

1. Weir, *Henry VIII: King and Court*
2. *CSP Venice*
3. Young, *Tudor and Jacobean Tournaments*
4. Hall, *Hall's Chronicle: Containing the history of England*
5. Samman, 'The Henrician court during Cardinal Wolsey's ascendancy c.1514-1529'

6. Hall, *Hall's Chronicle: Containing the history of England*
7. *Letters and Papers, Foreign and Domestic, Henry VIII*
8. *CSP Venice*
9. Hall, *Hall's Chronicle: Containing the history of England*
10. *Letters and Papers, Foreign and Domestic, Henry VIII*
11. Ibid.
12. Ibid.
13. Ibid.
14. Harris Nicolas, *History of the Orders of Knighthood of the British Empire*
15. *Letters and Papers, Foreign and Domestic, Henry VIII*
16. Nichols, *The Chronicle of Calais,*
17. *Letters and Papers, Foreign and Domestic, Henry VIII*
18. Ibid.
19. Ibid.
20. Fortescue, *Sir John Fortescue, Knight, His Life, Works, and Family History in Two Volumes*
21. Bindoff, *The House of Commons*

Chapter Three: A Soldier in Scotland

1. Stuart, *The Scot who was a Frenchman*
2. Hall, *Hall's Chronicle: Containing the history of England*
3. Ibid.
4. Ibid.
5. *Letters and Papers, Foreign and Domestic, Henry VIII*
6. Ibid.
7. Ibid.
8. Ibid.
9. Leland, *De Rebus Brittanicis Collectanea*
10. *Letters and Papers, Foreign and Domestic, Henry VIII*
11. Ibid.
12. Ibid.
13. Myers, *The Household of Edward IV*
14. Hall, *Hall's Chronicle: Containing the history of England*

15. Shulman, *Graven with Diamonds*

Chapter Four: A Changing World

1. *CSP Spain*
2. *Letters and Papers, Foreign and Domestic, Henry VIII*
3. Cavendish, *The Life and Death of Cardinal Wolsey*
4. *Letters and Papers, Foreign and Domestic, Henry VIII*
5. Ibid.
6. Ibid.
7. *CSP Spain*
8. *Letters and Papers, Foreign and Domestic, Henry VIII*
9. Ibid.
10. *CSP Venice*
11. *Letters and Papers, Foreign and Domestic, Henry VIII*
12. Ibid.
13. Ibid.
14. Ibid.
15. Ibid.
16. Ibid.
17. Ibid.
18. Ibid.
19. Ibid.
20. Ibid.
21. Ibid.
22. Ibid.
23. Ibid.
24. Ibid.
25. Ibid.
26. Brigden, *Thomas Wyatt*
27. *CSP Venice*
28. *Letters and Papers, Foreign and Domestic, Henry VIII*
29. Ibid.
30. Ibid.
31. Ibid.

32. Ellis, *Original Letters Illustrative of English History:*
33. *Letters and Papers, Foreign and Domestic, Henry VIII*

Chapter Five: Diplomatic Duties

1. García, 'Charles V and the Habsburgs' Inventories. Changing Patrimony as Dynastic Cult in Early Modern Europe'
2. *Letters and Papers, Foreign and Domestic, Henry VIII*
3. Ibid.
4. Ibid.
5. Ibid.
6. Ibid.
7. Ibid.
8. Cavendish, *The Life and Death of Cardinal Wolsey*
9. *Letters and Papers, Foreign and Domestic, Henry VIII*
10. Ibid.
11. *CSP Venice*
12. *Letters and Papers, Foreign and Domestic, Henry VIII*
13. Ibid.
14. Ibid.
15. Ibid.
16. Ibid.
17. Frieda, *Francis I*
18. *Letters and Papers, Foreign and Domestic, Henry VIII*
19. Ibid.
20. Ibid.
21. Ibid.
22. *CSP Spain*
23. *Letters and Papers, Foreign and Domestic, Henry VIII*
24. Ibid.
25. *CSP Spain*
26. Hall, *Hall's Chronicle: Containing the history of England*
27. Ibid.
28. *CSP Spain*
29. *Letters and Papers, Foreign and Domestic, Henry VIII*

30. Ibid.
31. St Clare Byrne, *The Lisle Letters*
32. *Letters and Papers, Foreign and Domestic, Henry VIII*
33. Ibid.
34. St Clare Byrne, *The Lisle Letters*
35. Ibid.
36. Ibid.
37. *Letters and Papers, Foreign and Domestic, Henry VIII*
38. St Clare Byrne, *The Lisle Letters*

Chapter Six: The Fall of a Queen

1. *Letters and Papers, Foreign and Domestic, Henry VIII*
2. St Clare Byrne, *The Lisle Letters*
3. Ibid.
4. Ibid.
5. Ibid.
6. Ibid.
7. Ibid.
8. *Letters and Papers, Foreign and Domestic, Henry VIII*
9. *CSP Spain*
10. *Letters and Papers, Foreign and Domestic, Henry VIII*
11. Bindoff, *The House of Commons*
12. *Letters and Papers, Foreign and Domestic, Henry VIII*
13. Ibid.
14. Ibid.
15. Ibid.
16. Ibid.
17. *CSP Spain*
18. Ibid.
19. Ibid.
20. Ibid.
21. Cavendish, *The Life and Death of Cardinal Wolsey*
22. Weir, *The Lady in the Tower*
23. *Letters and Papers, Foreign and Domestic, Henry VIII*

24. Weir, *The Lady in the Tower*
25. *Letters and Papers, Foreign and Domestic, Henry VIII*
26. Weir, *The Lady in the Tower*
27. Sander, *Rise and Growth of the Anglican Schism*
28. *Letters and Papers, Foreign and Domestic, Henry VIII*
29. *CSP Spain*
30. *Letters and Papers, Foreign and Domestic, Henry VIII*
31. Brigden, *Thomas Wyatt: The Heart's Forest*
32. *Letters and Papers, Foreign and Domestic, Henry VIII*
33. Brigden, *Thomas Wyatt: The Heart's Forest*
34. *Letters and Papers, Foreign and Domestic, Henry VIII*
35. Ibid.
36. Ibid.
37. Ibid.
38. Ibid.
39. Starkey, *Rivals in Power: Lives and Letters of the Great Tudor Dynasties*
40. *Letters and Papers, Foreign and Domestic, Henry VIII*
41. Ibid.
42. Dodds, *The Pilgrimage of Grace 1536–1537*
43. *Letters and Papers, Foreign and Domestic, Henry VIII*
44. Ibid.
45. Ibid.
46. Ibid.
47. Ibid.
48. Weir, *Henry VIII*

Chapter Seven: A Time of Ill Favour

1. Pole, *Pro ecclesiasticae unitatis defensione (Defence of the Unity of the Church)*
2. *Letters and Papers, Foreign and Domestic, Henry VIII*
3. *CSP Spain*
4. *Letters and Papers, Foreign and Domestic, Henry VIII*
5. Ibid.

6. Ibid.
7. St Clare Byrne, *The Lisle Letters*
8. Ibid.
9. Ibid.
10. *Letters and Papers, Foreign and Domestic, Henry VIII*
11. Ibid.
12. Ibid.
13. Ibid.
14. St Clare Byrne, *The Lisle Letters*
15. *Letters and Papers, Foreign and Domestic, Henry VIII*
16. Ibid.
17. St Clare Byrne, *The Lisle Letters*
18. Ibid.
19. Brigden, *Thomas Wyatt: The Heart's Forest*
20. *Letters and Papers, Foreign and Domestic, Henry VIII*
21. Ibid.
22. Ibid.
23. Ibid.
24. Ibid.
25. Ibid.
26. Ibid.
27. Ibid.
28. Ibid.
29. Ibid.
30. Ibid.
31. Ibid.
32. St Clare Byrne, *The Lisle Letters*

Chapter Eight: A Tale of Two Queens

1. *Letters and Papers, Foreign and Domestic, Henry VIII*
2. Weir, *Henry VIII*
3. *Letters and Papers, Foreign and Domestic, Henry VIII*
4. Ibid.
5. Ibid.

6. Ibid.
7. Ibid.
8. Ibid.
9. Hall, *Hall's Chronicle: Containing the history of England*
10. *Letters and Papers, Foreign and Domestic, Henry VIII*
11. Ibid.
12. Ibid.
13. Ibid.
14. Ibid.
15. St Clare Byrne, *The Lisle Letters*
16. *Letters and Papers, Foreign and Domestic, Henry VIII*
17. Saaler, *Anne of Cleves*
18. *CSP Spain*
19. St Clare Byrne, *The Lisle Letters*
20. Ibid.
21. Starkey, *Six Wives*
22. *Letters and Papers, Foreign and Domestic, Henry VIII*
23. *CSP Spain*
24. Wyatt, *Selected Poems*
25. Brigden, *Thomas Wyatt: The Heart's Forest*
26. *Letters and Papers, Foreign and Domestic, Henry VIII*
27. Lewis, *The Wars of the Roses: The Key Players in the Struggle for Supremacy*
28. *Letters and Papers, Foreign and Domestic, Henry VIII*
29. Ibid.
30. St Clare Byrne, *The Lisle Letters*
31. Shulman, *Graven with Diamonds*
32. *Letters and Papers, Foreign and Domestic, Henry VIII*
33. Ibid.
34. Brigg, *Hertfordshire Genealogist and Antiquary*
35. Ibid.
36. Ibid.

Chapter Nine: To War with France

1. *Letters and Papers, Foreign and Domestic, Henry VIII*
2. Loades, *John Dudley*
3. *Letters and Papers, Foreign and Domestic, Henry VIII*
4. Ibid.
5. Ibid.
6. Ibid.
7. Ibid.
8. Watkins, *Anne of Cleves*
9. Ibid.
10. *CSP Spain*
11. Ibid.
12. Carte, *A General History of England*
13. *Letters and Papers, Foreign and Domestic, Henry VIII*
14. Ibid.
15. Ibid.
16. Childs, *Henry VIII's Last Victim*
17. *Letters and Papers, Foreign and Domestic, Henry VIII*
18. Gruffydd, *Elis Gruffydd and the 1544 Enterprises of Paris and Boulogne*
19. Hall, *Hall's Chronicle: Containing the history of England*
20. Childs, *Henry VIII's Last Victim*
21. *Letters and Papers, Foreign and Domestic, Henry VIII*
22. Ibid.
23. Foxe, *History of the Acts and Monuments of the Church*
24. Ibid.
25. Ibid.
26. Bapst, *Two Gentleman Poets at the Court of Henry VIII: George Boleyn and Henry Howard*
27. *Letters and Papers, Foreign and Domestic, Henry VIII*
28. Bapst, *Two Gentleman Poets at the Court of Henry VIII: George Boleyn and Henry Howard*
29. *Letters and Papers, Foreign and Domestic, Henry VIII*
30. Sander, *Rise and Growth of the Anglican Schism*

Chapter Ten: Final Days in Ireland

1. *Letters and Papers, Foreign and Domestic, Henry VIII*
2. Patten, 'The Expedicion in Scotlande'
3. Skidmore, *Edward VI*
4. Pincombe, *The Oxford Handbook of Tudor Literature: 1485–1603*
5. Drayton, *Delphi Collected Works of Michael Drayton*
6. Drayton, *England's Heroical Epistles*
7. Meres, *Palladis Tamia*
8. Kirwan, 'Lady Joan FitzGerald, Countess of Ormond, Ossory, and Desmond' in *Journal of the Butler Society*, Volume 4
9. Ibid.
10. Ibid.
11. *CSP Ireland*
12. Brigden, *Thomas Wyatt: The Heart's Forest*
13. *Calendar of the Cecil Papers*
14. Kirwan, 'Lady Joan FitzGerald, Countess of Ormond, Ossory, and Desmond' in *Journal of the Butler Society*, Volume 4
15. *CSP Ireland*
16. *Calendar of the Cecil Papers*
17. Ibid.
18. Kirwan, 'Lady Joan FitzGerald, Countess of Ormond, Ossory, and Desmond' in *Journal of the Butler Society*, Volume 4
19. *CSP Ireland*
20. Fuller, *The Spear and Spindle*
21. *CSP Ireland*
22. Ibid.
23. Lefevre-Pontalis, *Political Correspondence of Odet de Selve*
24. Le Grand, *Histoire du Divorce de Henri VIII*

Appendix One

1. *Letters and Papers, Foreign and Domestic, Henry VIII*
2. Ibid.
3. Andrews, *A critical and historical review of Fox's Book of martyrs*

Acknowledgements

My sincere thanks for their help in many ways go to Robert Barrs-James, Stephen Dudley, the Rev. Canon Barbara Fryday and John Kirwan.

Bibliography

Andrews, William Eusebius, *A critical and historical review of Fox's Book of martyrs, shewing the inaccuracies, falsehoods, and misrepresentations in that work of deception*, London, 1824

Anglo, Sydney, *Spectacle Pageantry and Early Tudor Policy*, Oxford, 1969

Baldwin Smith, Lacey, *Treason in Tudor England*, London, 1986

Bapst, Edmond, translated by Ridgeway, Claire, *Two Gentleman Poets at the Court of Henry VIII: George Boleyn and Henry Howard*, 2003

Bernard, André, *The Life of Henry VII*, translated and introduced by Daniel Hobbins, New York, 2011

Bernard, G W, *Anne Boleyn: Fatal Attractions*, Yale, 2010

Bernard, G W, *The King's Reformation*, Yale, 2005

Bernard, G W, *The Tudor Nobility*, Manchester, 1992

Bindoff, Stanley, *The House of Commons 1509-1558*, Volume 1, London, 1982

BL Cotton Ms Caligula D. VI, f.149

Borman, Tracy, *Thomas Cromwell*, London, 2014

Brigden, Susan, *Thomas Wyatt: The Heart's Forest*, London, 2012

Briggs, W., *Hertfordshire Genealogist and Antiquary*, 1895-8

Bryan, Francis, *A dispraise of the life of a courtier, and a commendacion of the life of the labouryng man*, 1548

Calendar of the Cecil Papers in Hatfield House, London, 1883

Calendar of State Papers, Domestic (Edward, Mary and Elizabeth)

Calendar of State Papers, Foreign

Calendar of State Papers, France

Calendar of State Papers, Scotland

Calendar of State Papers, Spain

Calendar of State Papers, Venice

Cavendish, George, *The Life and Death of Cardinal Wolsey*, Massachusetts, 1905

Chapman, Hester, *The Sisters of Henry VIII*, Bath, 1969

Childs, Jessie, *Henry VIII's Last Victim*, London, 2008

Cripps-Day, F H, *The History of the Tournament in England and France*, London, 1918

Dodds, Madeleine Hope, *The Pilgrimage of Grace 1536–1537 and the Exeter Conspiracy 1538, Volume 1*, Cambridge, 2015

Drayton, Michael, *Delphi Collected Works of Michael Drayton*, ebook, 2015

Drayton, Michael, *England's Heroical Epistles*, London, 1798

Ellis, Henry, *Original Letters Illustrative of English History: Including Numerous Royal Letters and One or Two other Collections Volume II*, London, 1824

Ellis, Steven, *Tudor Ireland*, Harlow, 1985

Erickson, Carolly, *Great Harry: The Extravagant Life of Henry VIII*, London, 1997

Foster, *Athenae Oxonienses*

Foster, *Alumni Oxonienses 1500–1714*, Oxford, 1891

Fletcher, Catherine, *The Divorce of Henry VIII*, London, 2013

Fortescue, Thomas, *Sir John Fortescue, Knight, His Life, Works, and Family History in Two Volumes*, London, 1869

Foxe, John, *History of the Acts and Monuments of the Church (Foxe's Book of Martyrs)*, London, 1563

Fraser, Antonia, *The Six Wives of Henry VIII*, London, 1992

Freida, Leona, *Francis I*, London, 2018

Fuller, T. A., *The Spear and the Spindle*, Maryland, 2008

García, Juan Luis González, 'Charles V and the Habsburgs' Inventories. Changing Patrimony as Dynastic Cult in Early Modern Europe', *RIHA Journal* 0012, 11 November 2010

Grafton, Richard, *Grafton's Chronicle, Or History of England: To which is Added His Table of the Bailiffs, Sheriffs and Mayors of the City of London from the Year 1189, to 1558, Volumes 1 and 2*, London, 1809

Griffiths, R A, *The Making of the Tudor Dynasty*, Stroud, 2011

Gruffyd, Elis, *Elis Gruffydd and the 1544 Enterprises of Paris and*

Boulogne, Pike & Shot Society, 2003

Gunn, S J, *Charles Brandon, Duke of Suffolk 1484–1545*, Oxford, 1988

Gunn, S J, *The Duke of Suffolk's March on Paris in 1523*, English *Historical Review*, Vol. 101, No. 400 (Jul., 1986), pp. 596–634

Hall, Edward, *Hall's Chronicle: Containing the history of England*, ed. H. Ellis, London, 1809

Harris Nicolas, Nicholas, *History of the Orders of Knighthood of the British Empire; of the Order of the Guelphs of Hanover; and of the Medals, Clasps, and Crosses, Conferred for Naval and Military Services, Volume 1*, London, 1842

Head, David, *The Ebbs and Flows of Fortune: The Life of Thomas Howard, Third Duke of Norfolk*, Athens, 2009

Holinshed, Raphael, *Chronicles of England, Scotland and Ireland*, London, 1807

Hutchinson, Robert, *House of Treason: The Rise and Fall of the Tudor Dynasty*, London, 2009

Ives, Eric, *The Life and Death of Anne Boleyn*, London, 2005

Journals of The Butler Society, Vol. 3 No.4, Vol.4 No.1, Vol.4 No. 2

Knecht, R J, *Francis I*, Cambridge, 1982

Lefevre-Pontalis, Germain, *Political Correspondence of Odet de Selve*, Paris, 1888

Le Grand, Joachim, *Histoire du Divorce de Henri VIII*, Paris, 1688

Leland, *De Rebus Brittanicis Collectanea Vol 5*, London, 1774

Letters and Papers, Foreign and Domestic, Henry VIII

Lewis, Matthew, *The Wars of the Roses: The Key Players in the Struggle for Supremacy*, Stroud, 2015

Loades, David, *Henry VIII: Court, church and conflict*, The National Archives, 2007

Loades, David, *Henry VIII: King and Court*, Andover, 2009

Loughlin, Susan, *Insurrection*, Stroud, 2016

Mackay, Lauren, *Inside the Tudor Court*, Stroud, 2014

Mathusiak, John, *Henry VIII*, Stroud, 2013

Mattingly, Garrett, *Catherine of Aragon*, New York, 1941

Meres, Francis, *Palladis Tamia: Wit's Treasury*, London, 1598

Merriman, R B, *Life and Letters of Thomas Cromwell*, Oxford, 1902

Moorhouse, Geoffrey, *The Pilgrimage of Grace*, London, 2002

Mueller, J, ed., *Katherine Parr: Complete Works and Correspondence*, Chicago, 2011

Myers, Alec, ed., The Household of Edward IV, Manchester, 1959

Nichols, John Gough, *The Chronicle of Calais, in the reigns of Henry VII and Henry VIII to the year 1540*, J. B. Nichols and Son, 1846

Parmiter, Geoffrey de C, *The King's Great Matter*, London, 1967

Patten, 'The Expedicion into Scotlande', printed in *Fragments of Scottish History*, Edinburgh, 1798

Pincombe, Mike (ed.), *The Oxford Handbook of Tudor Literature: 1485-1603*, Oxford, 2009

Pole, Reginald, *Pro ecclesiasticae unitatis defensione* (*Defence of the Unity of the Church*), 1536

Porter, Linda, *Katherine the Queen*, London, 2010

Rappaport, Steve, *Worlds Within Worlds: Structures of Life in Sixteenth-Century London*, Cambridge, 2002

Rogers, E, ed., *Correspondence of Thomas More*, Princeton, 1947

Russell, Gareth, *Young, Damned and Fair: The Life and Tragedy of Catherine Howard at the Court of Henry VIII*, London, 2017

Saaler, Mary, *Anne of Cleves*, London, 1995

Samman, Neil, 'The Henrician court during Cardinal Wolsey's ascendancy c.1514–1529', University of Wales Ph.D, 1988

Sander, Nicholas, *Rise and Growth of the Anglican Schism*, London, 1877

Scarisbrick, J J, *Henry VIII*, London, 1997

Sharpe, Kevin, *Selling the Tudor Monarchy: Authority and Image in Sixteenth Century England*, Yale, 2009

Shulman, Nicola, *Graven with Diamonds: The Many Lives of Thomas Wyatt*, London, 2011

Sim, Alison, *Masters and Servants in Tudor England*, Stroud, 2006

Skidmore, Chris, *Edward VI*, London, 2008

Starkey, David, *The Reign of Henry VIII*, London, 1985

Starkey, David, ed., *Rivals in Power: Lives and Letters of the Great Tudor Dynasties*, London, 1990

Starkey, David, *Six Wives: The Queens of Henry VIII*, London, 2003

St Clare Byrne, Muriel, ed., *The Lisle Letters*, Chicago, 1981

Strype, *Ecclesiastical Memorials of Henry VIII, Edward VI and Mary*, London, 1816

Stuart, Marie W., *The Scot who was a Frenchman*, London, 1940

Thomas, A H and Thornley, I D, eds,. *Great Chronicle of London*, London, 1938

Vergil, Polydore, *Anglica Historia*, ed. Hay, Camden Society, 1950

Warnicke, Retha, *The Rise and Fall of Anne Boleyn: Family Politics at the Court of Henry VIII*, Cambridge, 1991

Watkins, Sarah-Beth, *Anne of Cleves: Henry VIII's Unwanted Wife*, Winchester, 2018

Weir, Alison, *The Lady in the Tower*, London, 2010

Weir, Alison, *The Six Wives of Henry VIII*, London, 1991

Weir, Alison, *Henry VIII: King and Court*, London, 2008

Wood, Anthony, *Athenae Oxonienses*, London, 1813

Wyatt, Sir Thomas, *Selected Poems of Sir Thomas Wyatt*, London, 2013

Young, Alan, *Tudor and Jacobean Tournaments*, London, 1987

CHRONOS
BOOKS

HISTORY

Chronos Books is an historical non-fiction imprint. Chronos
publishes real history for real people; bringing to life people,
places and events in an imaginative, easy-to-digest and
accessible way - histories that pass on their stories to a
generation of new readers.
If you have enjoyed this book, why not tell other readers by
posting a review on your preferred book site.

Recent bestsellers from Chronos Books are:

Lady Katherine Knollys
The Unacknowledged Daughter of King Henry VIII
Sarah-Beth Watkins
A comprehensive account of Katherine Knollys' questionable paternity, her previously unexplored life in the Tudor court and her intriguing relationship with Elizabeth I.
Paperback: 978-1-78279-585-8 ebook: 978-1-78279-584-1

Cromwell was Framed
Ireland 1649
Tom Reilly
Revealed: The definitive research that proves the Irish nation owes Oliver Cromwell a huge posthumous apology for wrongly convicting him of civilian atrocities in 1649.
Paperback: 978-1-78279-516-2 ebook: 978-1-78279-515-5

Why The CIA Killed JFK and Malcolm X
The Secret Drug Trade in Laos
John Koerner
A new groundbreaking work presenting evidence that the CIA silenced JFK to protect its secret drug trade in Laos.
Paperback: 978-1-78279-701-2 ebook: 978-1-78279-700-5

The Disappearing Ninth Legion
A Popular History
Mark Olly
The Disappearing Ninth Legion examines hard evidence for the foundation, development, mysterious disappearance, or possible continuation of Rome's lost Legion.
Paperback: 978-1-84694-559-5 ebook: 978-1-84694-931-9

Readers of ebooks can buy or view any of these bestsellers by clicking on the live link in the title. Most titles are published in paperback and as an ebook. Paperbacks are available in traditional bookshops. Both print and ebook formats are available online.

Find more titles and sign up to our readers' newsletter at
http://www.johnhuntpublishing.com/history-home

Follow us on Facebook at
https://www.facebook.com/ChronosBooks

and Twitter at https://twitter.com/ChronosBooks